MOSSAD'S TOP-SECRET MISSIONS EXPOSED

Secrets of Israel's Elite Intelligence Agency

Prabal Jain

Riverwood Capital

ISBN: 9798867520229

CONTENTS

PART I

INTRODUCTION

In the world of intelligence and covert operations, one agency stands out for its mystique and impact on global affairs - Mossad. This book delves into the enigmatic history of Mossad, peeling back the layers of secrecy to reveal a story of daring missions and complex geopolitics.

Mossad's mission is as clear as it is challenging: to safeguard Israel and prevent another Holocaust. From its inception in the post-World War II era, Mossad has evolved into one of the world's most effective intelligence agencies, driven by a resolute commitment to Israel's security.

The pages that follow will unveil Mossad's influence on the world stage. From high-stakes operations like the assassination of Iranian nuclear scientists to its involvement in shaping global politics, Mossad's actions have left an indelible mark on history.

For over five decades, Mossad has been a key player in the Middle East's most significant events. Feared and powerful, it has also sparked controversy and ethical debates. We will explore the agency's pivotal role in events such as the Dubai operation and consider the moral dilemmas it raises.

Join us on a journey through the shadowy world of Mossad.

This book is designed to provide a comprehensive yet accessible account of its operations and their implications, regardless of your background in intelligence and espionage.

CHAPTER 1: SHADOWS OF ESPIONAGE

In the tumultuous world of espionage, Mossad emerged as a hidden sword, crafted to safeguard Israel's very existence. Since its birth, the Jewish state has been locked in a relentless struggle against neighboring nations that denied its right to survive. And in this battle for survival, Mossad was entrusted with a task that transcends borders and defies the light of day - waging an invisible war.

Imagine a world where shadows hold secrets more potent than daylight. Mossad, the enigmatic intelligence agency, thrives in this realm, where clandestine operations, surveillance, assassinations, and sabotage are the tools of the trade. From the haunting echoes of the Holocaust to the ever-present specter of security threats, Mossad has but one directive: "rise and kill first." These are the unsung heroes, the nameless faces, risking their lives to ensure the safety of Israel. Theirs is a world where silence speaks volumes and every action has a consequence, be it in the quiet of a room or the chaos of the field.

And then there was Dubai. The mission was only a partial success, yet it exemplified Mossad's unwavering resolve. Mahmoud al-Mabhouh's liquidation went off without a hitch, but it also pulled Mossad out of the shadows and into the harsh glare of the international stage. The agents barely slipped through the fingers of Dubai's law enforcement, and Mossad's involvement was vehemently, albeit with a touch of reluctance, denied. This was no Hollywood thriller, but a real-world tale of espionage that tantalizingly tingles the senses. The Israeli government's response, neither confirming nor denying its role, left room for speculation and conspiracy theories to bloom. The line between fact and fiction blurred as intrigue gripped the global imagination.

But let's peel back the layers of movie glamor. The world of intelligence is intricate, where gray areas far outweigh the black and white. In the midst of near failure in Dubai, Mossad's message was clear - Israel's reach is long, and it would stop at nothing to secure its future.

Mossad's mystique is carefully cultivated, a weapon in itself. It is both a myth and a deterrent, a legend that deters potential adversaries. And it's not just about espionage; it's about power and politics, and how actions echo in the corridors of international power.

CHAPTER 2: ORIGINS OF SHADOWS

In the hidden annals of the intelligence world, one theory continues to reverberate - the belief, held by some in the Arab world, that Mossad's influence extended to the cataclysmic events of 9/11. While this theory might appear steeped in conspiracy, it underscores the enigmatic aura that envelops Mossad.

Mossad never set out to become a legend; it was a byproduct of their unwavering commitment to clandestine secret espionage and operational work. Over time, they recognized that this myth served them well, amplifying their influence on the world stage.

Officially known as the "Institute for Information and Special Operations," Mossad has been charged with the sacred duty of protecting Israel from harm since 1951. In the process, Mossad has become a household name across the globe, a testament to its audacious exploits that have catapulted it into the realm of the most publicized secret services.

Despite its notoriety, Mossad operates with a surprisingly lean team, employing a mere 3,000 people. A David in the world of espionage when compared to the Goliath of the CIA, which can call on up to 23,000 operatives. However, when measured in the context of the countries' respective populations, Mossad stands as a giant, about five times more substantial than its American counterpart.

Israel's investment in Mossad's capabilities is substantial. The value of discrete and well-targeted security measures became evident early on. It's a testament to the importance of intelligence services, helping to forestall attacks and shape political developments.

The origins of Israel's secret services can be traced back to the Jewish underground activities in Ottoman Palestine towards the end of the 19th century. As the first Jewish immigrants from Europe set foot on the land of their forefathers, then under Turkish rule, a tumultuous chapter in history unfolded.

In 1917, during World War I, British troops ousted their Turkish opponents and pledged to create a Jewish state after the war. However, the Arabs had also been promised a state of their own one year earlier. This intricate web of promises set the stage for decades of conflict.

As the Jewish community acquired extensive stretches of land in Palestine, their settlements faced relentless attacks by outraged Arabs. In response, a clandestine movement emerged - a movement with a dual purpose. It sought to strike back and, simultaneously, prepare for the eventual formation of a Jewish state.

At the heart of this early phase of Israel's history was the realization that the Jewish population in Palestine was a minority, with limited military forces at its disposal. Thus, the acquisition of intelligence and information became a pivotal asset. Information was not only instrumental in winning wars but also in securing peace, a principle that holds true to this day.

CHAPTER 3: THE CRUCIBLE OF CONFLICT

In the turbulent crucible of Palestine's history, information and intelligence became invaluable assets. These tools held the power to tip the scales, not only in the heat of battle but also in the pursuit of lasting peace. Today, intelligence services remain as vital to Israel as they were in the formative years, serving to preempt attacks and shape the nation's political destiny.

The Jewish underground organization known as Haganah played a central role during these tumultuous times. Operating a network of informers among Arabs and Britons alike, they sought to gain a strategic advantage through intelligence. But Haganah's ambitions extended beyond intelligence; they smuggled guns into Palestine and aided Jewish immigrants fleeing the horrors of Nazi-occupied Europe. Britain, as the mandatory power in Palestine, sought to control immigration in an effort to appease the Arab population. Yet, in the face of the Holocaust and the increasing influx of Jewish refugees from Europe, an irresistible urge for refuge in the Middle East took hold.

Mossad, despite its later notoriety, had humble beginnings. Many of its agents cut their teeth in the ranks of Haganah. One such veteran was Shmuel Goren, whose early experiences in the clandestine world would shape the future of Mossad.

Goren reminisces about a daring Molotov cocktail attack in Haifa that led to his arrest. Inside his pocket, the police discovered a pistol, landing him in a British police station for three days.

However, the tide was turning. Jewish infiltrators within the security forces proved advantageous. These individuals could pull strings, turning the wheels of fate.

As World War II drew to a close, the situation in Palestine grew increasingly dire. Hundreds of thousands of Holocaust survivors, in search of a safe haven, were met with unyielding restrictions on immigration imposed by Great Britain. Frustration and determination grew hand in hand among Jewish activists, now more resolute than ever to fight for an independent Jewish state that could provide sanctuary to their kin.

It was in this charged atmosphere that radical splinter groups emerged, boldly targeting British institutions. Among their leaders was Menachem Begin, a future Prime Minister of Israel. Their audacious act of blowing up the King David Hotel in Jerusalem, the British administrative headquarters, left 91 people dead.

In 1947, Britain's announcement of its withdrawal from its mandate in Palestine, combined with the United Nations' decision to partition the land, painted a portrait of hope and despair. The vision of a Jewish state had become a reality, with nearly a third of Palestine's population being Jewish. Yet, the UN resolution that sanctioned this transformation would cast a long shadow.

The Crucible Of War

The immediate consequence of this momentous decision was an irregular war, one born out of a determined resolve by the Arab world to thwart the establishment of a Jewish state. Surrounding nations lent their unwavering support to the Palestinian cause, fueling the flames of conflict. The hour of Haganah had returned. Back in the 1920s, David Ben-Gurion, the future first Secretary of Defense and Prime Minister of Israel, played a pivotal role in raising Haganah. His vision and leadership would prove instrumental in the challenging days that lay ahead.

The proclamation of the state of Israel on May 14, 1948, served as a catalyst, triggering a swift and unrelenting military response by its Arab neighbors. That same night, six Arab states declared war on Israel, converging on three fronts with the singular objective of crushing the fledgling Jewish state once and for all. On paper, the Arab alliance boasted overwhelming troop strength and superior equipment, but their soldiers were inexperienced in the ways of conventional warfare. In contrast, the former underground fighters of Haganah were battle-hardened, well-organized, and highly motivated. Their mastery lay in achieving maximum effects with limited means.

In 1948, Israel's population was just around 650,000, a demographic minnow compared to the surrounding Arab states. David Ben-Gurion, acutely aware of Israel's resource constraints and relative weakness, recognized that intelligence could be a formidable force multiplier. Intelligence wasn't just about forewarning; it was equally about carrying out strategic operations that could tip the scales in favor of the nascent state. For Israel, intelligence became a linchpin in their struggle for survival. On the other side of the battlefield, the Arab rulers were driven primarily by their own interests, often at the expense of a unified strategy.

By July 1949, Israel emerged victorious in its first war against its neighbors. The prime lesson drawn from this conflict was clear - intelligence about the enemy was a war-winning factor. In the chapters ahead, we will continue to journey through the corridors of espionage, exploring the pivotal role intelligence played in the early years of Israel's statehood.

◆ ◆ ◆

CHAPTER 4: THE BIRTH OF THE ISRAELI INTELLIGENCE APPARATUS

Former homes of the German Templars, a Christian group, located in Tel Aviv, became the first headquarters in the immediate vicinity of the government led by David Ben-Gurion. Today, Israel boasts three distinct intelligence agencies, with Mossad taking the lead, both in terms of staff and budget. Mossad's mandate extends beyond Israel's borders, focused on safeguarding not only its citizens but Jews worldwide.

The early years of these intelligence agencies were marked by relentless pressure, rapid expansion, and the constant need for improvisation. Among the first operatives were former underground fighters like Shmuel Goren, who grappled with the challenge of starting everything from scratch. There was no blueprint, no manual on how to run this kind of operation. They had to adapt to the new reality, and they did so amid numerous challenges.

From the outset, Israel's spies were not limited to intelligence gathering; they were also tasked with executing special operations. This strategy was born from the principles of irregular warfare, designed to weaken the enemy without risking full-scale confrontation. The young Jewish state needed to conserve its resources, and Mossad emerged as the vanguard of this policy.

Isser Harel, the head of Mossad since 1952, went even further, recruiting former radical underground fighters who had been declared enemies of David Ben-Gurion. He offered them a chance at a legitimate existence, far removed from political activism. Some of these recruits had earned their reputation as tough killers, experienced in the murky world of terrorism and assassinations.

In the chapters that follow, we will continue to delve into the growth and evolution of Israeli intelligence agencies, the challenges they faced, and the morally complex decisions they had to make in the quest to ensure the survival and prosperity of the Jewish state.

The Veil of Secrecy

Ben-Gurion, while speaking about democracy, found himself teetering on a precipice. He was no executioner of democracy, but the relentless pressures of a region embroiled in conflict compelled him to make tough decisions. One of those decisions was the uncompromising demand for 100% secrecy in the newly established intelligence community. In this shadowy world, organizations were not even named, their existence denied to all.

The state of emergency declared by Ben-Gurion in 1948 still lingered like a haunting specter. For Israel's forces and Mossad, this meant a delicate balancing act. They had to act in accordance with democratic rules and the law, all while safeguarding the nation's security. However, in the realm of clandestine espionage, procuring sensitive data often involves breaching the laws of the countries involved.

Every intelligence service grapples with a perennial question: Is the risk justified by the reward? In Israel, the answer to this question differed from that in many Western or Central European services. The pressure on Mossad was relentless; it had to prove its worth in safeguarding Israel. This meant taking more significant risks than their Western counterparts.

This clandestine journey had left an indelible mark on Mossad. For years, it operated successfully behind the curtain, executing covert operations shrouded in secrecy. Until one fateful night, an audacious mission would expose its prowess to the world.

CHAPTER 5: THE HUNT FOR THE ARCHITECT OF EVIL

It was 1961, and the stage was set in Jerusalem for one of the most significant trials in history. In the dock was Adolf Eichmann, the man who had orchestrated the Holocaust, a man whose name had become synonymous with pure evil. Just a year earlier, Mossad agents had pulled off a sensational coup by kidnapping the former SS officer from his hiding place in Argentina.

Eichmann, one of the key organizers of the Holocaust, had managed to escape justice after the war, seeking refuge in Buenos Aires. There, he lived under a false identity, his existence shrouded in secrecy. However, when Mossad received a tip about his whereabouts, they acted swiftly. A team of 67 agents was dispatched to South America, with Mossad agent Rafi Eitan leading the operation.

In a tense hideout near Eichmann's home, Eitan and his team confronted the architect of evil. Eitan's firm grip and a swift maneuver brought Eichmann to the ground, and he was whisked into a car. The first question posed to Eichmann was simple: "What's your name?" The response, "Ricardo Clement," was the name he had lived under in Argentina. But a few seconds later, he made a chilling admission. "I've been expecting this moment day and night. I knew you Israelis would find me someday."

Eichmann's capture had presented a chilling choice. It wouldn't have been difficult to put a few bullets in his head right then and there, eliminating the threat and reducing the risk. However,

David Ben-Gurion had been clear in his orders: Eichmann must be brought to trial. "This is not the law of the jungle," Ben-Gurion insisted.

The operation to apprehend Eichmann was not without controversy. Many Holocaust survivors had accused Ben-Gurion of displaying too little interest in their suffering, and hunting down Nazis was not a top priority for the Israeli government. After the war, no announcements were made about Israel actively seeking out Nazis, and the country had only recently begun to establish official relations with West Germany.

Shadows of the Past and the Eichmann Trial

In the complex world of international diplomacy, pragmatism often takes precedence. Israel and West Germany were at the threshold of establishing official relations, a crucial step for two young nations eager to move beyond their shared, painful history.

However, within the cabinet of German Chancellor Konrad Adenauer, there was a lingering issue. Hans Globke, head of the federal chancellery, had a Nazi past that could prove problematic, especially during the Eichmann trial. Eichmann had been in some form of contact with Globke, and the latter was aware of Eichmann's presence in Argentina. Those who had remained in the executive branch of West Germany understandably didn't want their dark pasts unearthed.

The German government pressed for Globke's name to be left out of the Eichmann trial. Unbeknownst to many, both Germany's Federal Intelligence Service (BND) and the CIA had been well aware of Eichmann's hideout in Argentina. Yet, the fact that Mossad, an Israeli agency, had successfully captured a leading Nazi criminal bolstered Israeli self-confidence.

The capture of Adolf Eichmann stands as one of Mossad's greatest triumphs, even though Mossad director Isser Harel had been informed of Eichmann's whereabouts several years earlier. At the time, Harel hadn't recognized the operation's full potential. Only later did he grasp the magnitude of the publicity and myth it could create.

The Eichmann trial unfolded on the world stage, becoming the cornerstone of Mossad's legend. It sent a powerful message to Israel's enemies: Mossad agents might strike anywhere. It was a moment of profound pride for the Jewish people, a declaration that they had survived and prevailed despite the horrors of the Holocaust.

Following Eichmann's capture, only one other Nazi criminal was apprehended by Mossad. In the 1960s, Mossad agents embarked on a series of daring and risky infiltrations into Israel's Arab neighbors. The premise was simple: another attack on the Jewish state might be imminent at any time. Since 1949, Israel had occupied land assigned to the Palestinians by the United Nations, a contentious issue that further fueled tensions in the region.

Mossad's operatives employed sophisticated cover stories, enabling them to access the highest echelons of their Arab adversaries. From these vantage points, they recruited additional agents and informers, often with the voluntary support of local Jewish communities. Inside the secretive halls of Mossad's headquarters in Tel Aviv, a web of intrigue and espionage continued to evolve, shaped by the lessons of history and the imperatives of the present.

CHAPTER 6: SHADOWS
IN HIGH SOCIETY

Within the clandestine world of Mossad, agents were trained for missions abroad. They had a unique advantage—potential recruits were relatively easy to find in Israel. The country was a melting pot of immigrants who had left their countries of origin recently. People from all corners of the world were drawn to Israel, making it relatively straightforward to take someone from, say, Germany or Egypt and send them back as undercover agents.

Many of these immigrants, driven by a strong sense of idealism, were willing to serve Mossad and their new homeland. The salaries were meager, and the risks were colossal. Each agent knew that if they were arrested, they would face extensive torture and painful deaths.

In 1961, Mossad achieved a remarkable feat: they planted an agent in the upper echelons of Cairo's high society. Egypt, Israel's arch-enemy, was now being spied upon by a man posing as a German horse breeder. In reality, this man was an Israeli citizen named Wolfgang Lotz, born in Mannheim in 1921. Lotz had a distinct advantage in that he had not been circumcised, as he was born to a Jewish mother and a Christian father. He had immigrated to Palestine when the Nazis came to power in 1933 and had fought alongside the nascent IDF in the War of Independence. With this background, he was well-suited to create an undercover identity as a former German veterinary officer in the Afrika Korps.

The BND, Germany's Federal Intelligence Service, played a pivotal role in crafting Lotz's cover story. He spent several months in Germany, meticulously preparing for his role as a veteran of the Wehrmacht. In return, he would gather intelligence on die-hard Nazis in Egypt, an invaluable asset for Mossad.

The High Stakes Of Espionage In Egypt

Wolfgang Lotz's daring infiltration into Cairo's high society had paid off, thanks in no small part to the cooperation between Mossad and the BND. When he was arrested in 1965, the careful agreement between these intelligence services saved his life. Even after his cover was blown, both agencies shielded his true identity, leading to a remarkably lenient sentence for espionage and other criminal activities in Egypt. Soon after, Lotz was quietly repatriated to Germany.

As an ostensibly German spy, Lotz was sentenced to life imprisonment in 1972, but he eventually chose to reveal his story to the press. This revelation further contributed to the myth surrounding Mossad, cementing its reputation as a force to be reckoned with.

Had the Egyptians known that Lotz was a Mossad agent, he would have faced the death penalty. The same year, another Mossad agent met a far grimmer fate. Eli Cohen, who had posed as a wealthy businessman in Damascus while successfully spying on the Syrian military leadership, was arrested by the Syrians. In contrast to Lotz, Cohen paid the ultimate price, facing public execution.

Following the capture and execution of Eli Cohen, Mossad reevaluated its approach. They became more cautious about deploying their agents to target countries, shifting their focus to recruiting local agents instead. It became clear that securing sources within Arab states was less challenging than initially thought. Mossad's spymasters started overseeing their human assets from a safe distance, often providing them with substantial financial rewards as an incentive for their treacherous work.

CHAPTER 7: THREAT FROM EGYPTIAN MISSILE PROGRAM

Espionage in the world of Mossad often comes with immense risks, especially when their operatives must operate undercover, concealing their Israeli identities. In many instances, money proves to be the decisive incentive for potential informants. The reputation of Mossad can also play a crucial role in persuading individuals to cooperate. Some approach agents with inquiries, like how they can join Mossad, and the organization invests heavily in cultivating its informants, promising them protection wherever possible.

As a result, there are numerous business-like relationships where money is exchanged for intelligence, often spanning decades. While having well-placed human sources is invaluable, it must be complemented by the complex task of processing vast amounts of information to identify emerging threats. This challenge remains paramount, as Mossad sometimes finds itself blind to unfolding events, just as it did in the summer of 1962.

During that period, Israel faced an unforeseen threat from Egypt's President, Gamal Abdul Nasser. He proudly unveiled his new missiles, claiming they could reach Israel. Mossad agent Wolfgang Lotz had not reported any dramatic progress in the Egyptian missile program, leaving Mossad deeply concerned.

The situation was not without tension. Nasser's missile program relied heavily on German experts who had been involved in developing Hitler's V2 rockets. Despite their Nazi pasts, their involvement in Egypt's missile program continued. In the early decades after Israel's establishment, the fear of another Holocaust loomed large. Mossad recognized the urgent need to act and halt Nasser's rocket program.

The logistics of the program were overseen by Heinz Krug, a German lawyer and arms dealer who had moved to Cairo in the early 1960s. In total, 35 Germans were involved in NASA's missile project, and this collaboration was not a secret. They spoke openly about their work, with no one stopping them from mentioning it.

Both the Israeli and German governments were aware of the presence of their citizens in Cairo, but they had not taken any action against it. However, Mossad soon realized that the success of NASA's missile program heavily depended on the expertise of these German specialists.

To disrupt the program, Mossad initially attempted to eliminate key figures through parcel bombs, which resulted in the deaths of five Egyptian workers and the blinding of a German secretary, Hanna Lora Venda. However, Mossad eventually shifted its strategy, focusing on operations against the missile experts in West Germany.

Heinz Krug, who had played a significant role in organizing the logistical aspects of the missile program, became a prime target. On the morning of September 23, 1962, Heinz Krug left his family's flat for his office. Little did he know that this would be the last time he saw his daughter, Beata.

The Hunt for Otto Skorzeny

Mossad was on a relentless mission to thwart President Nasser's missile program. The involvement of former Nazi scientists in Egypt's missile development, including key figures like Heinz

Krug, raised deep concerns in Israel. While initial attempts to eliminate these experts had failed, Mossad sought new avenues.

In May 1964, Mossad identified an opportunity in Otto Skorzeny, a former SS officer who enjoyed the protection of Spanish dictator Francisco Franco. Skorzeny, one of the most prominent surviving Nazis, had direct access to the leading figures of Egypt's missile program. Mossad believed that recruiting him as an informant could provide critical insights.

However, the task was not without its challenges. When the idea of recruiting Skorzeny was proposed, Mossad's head of operations expressed skepticism, making a metaphorical statement that he'd believe it when he saw a sprout growing from the palm of his hand. The risks were significant, especially considering the recent international attention on Mossad's capture of Adolf Eichmann.

Skorzeny, who had been involved in high-profile operations during World War II, was rumored to be a target of those seeking retribution for Nazi war crimes. Mossad had successfully apprehended Eichmann, and the world was keenly watching their every move.

To convince Skorzeny to cooperate, Mossad needed a persuasive approach. While Skorzeny's life in Spain was comfortable, there were rumblings that those who had kidnapped Eichmann might be after him next. Mossad seized this opportunity and made contact with Skorzeny, seeking to recruit him as an informant.

The story of Mossad's quest to turn a prominent Nazi figure into an informant showcases the agency's bold and unrelenting pursuit of its objectives, even in the face of complex challenges and moral dilemmas.

CHAPTER 8: THE COLD WAR
IN THE MIDDLE EAST

As the 1960s progressed, the Cold War between the United States and the Soviet Union extended its reach into the Middle East, bringing about a new phase in the ongoing struggle for the Holy Land. The missile threat posed by Egypt's President Nasser had been successfully neutralized, but a new challenge emerged.

Israeli intelligence services, including Mossad, began to notice a growing influx of Soviet weapons and instructors into the Arab countries surrounding Israel. Moscow was determined to gain a foothold in the Middle East, aiming to weaken NATO's Southern flank. The conflict between the East and West was influencing global politics, and the Middle East had become a critical battleground.

In this geopolitical landscape, Israel found itself in a unique position. It was both a valuable ally for the United States, which sought to counter Soviet influence, and a nation that could benefit from Western support to keep Soviet power at bay in the region. The Cold War's global dynamics had drawn Israel into a complex web of alliances and intelligence cooperation.

Mossad, with its extensive contacts in the Arab world, became an essential asset for the Americans, who were considering entering the Middle Eastern arena. Cooperation with other intelligence services and the exchange of information remained central to Mossad's mission.

One of the key partnerships that developed was between Mossad and German Federal Intelligence, which provided logistical support. Agents from both countries could move relatively freely in Arab countries. The cooperation with other Western intelligence services, including the Americans, proved invaluable for Israel.

Shifting Alliances

The intricacies of intelligence cooperation in the midst of the Cold War become increasingly apparent as the story unfolds. Mossad's role as a global player in the world of espionage, negotiation, and information gathering takes center stage.

The focus shifts to the relentless pursuit of information and Mossad's interactions with various intelligence services, especially those of the United States and Germany. It becomes evident that working with these agencies means facing tough and persistent efforts to elicit valuable intelligence. Meetings with Mossad involve more than pleasant meals; they involve pressing for information that could serve Israel's interests. The mistrust that permeates these alliances highlights the delicate balance of power and mutual objectives.

Foreign, seeking cooperation with American secret services, finds itself in a precarious position. The United States was initially skeptical of Israel's role in the Cold War, with concerns about its socialist leadership and the origins of many of its citizens. The role of James Angleton, a CIA figure with connections to Israeli intelligence operatives from World War II, becomes pivotal. Angleton's transformation from an anti-Semite to a dedicated Zionist alters the dynamics. He passionately defends Israeli interests in American discussions, and Israel reciprocates by assisting the United States.

A significant turning point in their relations occurs in Warsaw when Victor Grebski, a Polish Jew, stumbles upon a well-kept secret. The transcript of a speech by Soviet leader Nikita Khrushchev falls into Israeli hands, who recognize its immense value. They share this critical piece of information with the CIA.

The evolving alliances and collaborations against the backdrop of the Cold War intensify the intrigue, placing Israel, and by extension Mossad, at the center of a complex geopolitical landscape.

The next part of the story delves into the implications of the information found in the Khrushchev speech and how it shapes international relations in the Cold War era.

CHAPTER 9: OPERATION DIAMOND TRIUMPH

As the 1960s unfold, a new danger looms on the horizon for Israel: the Soviet Union's growing influence in the Middle East. The delivery of modern combat jets to the surrounding Arab states, particularly the feared MiG-21, raises concerns. Mossad recognizes the need to understand these capabilities better and embarks on a daring plan.

Mossad's scheme to find an Arab pilot willing to defect and fly his MiG-21 to Israel. The prospect of gaining valuable insights into this advanced Soviet aircraft is too tempting to resist. Munir Redfur, a fighter pilot in the Iraqi Air Force, emerges as a promising candidate.

Redfur's frustration within the Iraqi Air Force due to his Assyrian Christian background becomes the fulcrum for Mossad's strategy. They skillfully approach him, recognizing his discontent and offering financial incentives. Mossad agents conduct their initial meetings with Redfur, keenly aware of his vulnerabilities.

The tension builds as Redfur contemplates the risky proposition. The Mossad agents raise the stakes, suggesting that he should defect with the MiG-21. The danger of being captured and executed is ever-present, no matter where he flies, and Mossad emphasizes the prospect of sanctuary in a friendly country.

A Risky Scheme

Negotiations unfold as Redfur considers the perilous mission. He insists on one condition: his family must be secretly smuggled out of Iraq to protect them from reprisals. Mossad, however, underestimated the extent of the Iraqi concept of family, as it extended to numerous relatives.

By mid-summer 1966, all preparations were in place. Redfur peels off during a training flight, guiding his fully armed MiG-21 to Israel. The operation is a resounding success. For the first time, a MiG-21 is in Western hands, and other intelligence agencies eagerly seek access to the results of Operation Diamond.

The chapter highlights how Mossad's strategic successes, like Operation Diamond, bolster Israel's position in the Western intelligence community. The benefits of this achievement become evident during the Six-Day War, where Israeli pilots, equipped with the knowledge gleaned from Redfur's MiG-21, outperform their Arab adversaries, achieving a remarkable five-to-one kill ratio.

Historians and military experts concur that Israeli intelligence played a pivotal role in the swift victory of the Six-Day War. This transformative conflict changes the dynamics of the region, amplifying the myths and legends surrounding Israeli intelligence and projecting a newfound sense of Israeli self-security. However, it also sets the stage for the simmering tensions and hostilities that will continue to shape the Middle East and define the challenges faced by Israeli intelligence.

CONCLUSION

Shaping Destiny, Forging Legends

In the annals of espionage, few agencies have etched their legacy as indelibly as Mossad, the Israeli intelligence service. From its humble beginnings to its meteoric rise, this book has chronicled Mossad's journey through the turbulent waters of history.

Mossad's early years, marked by daring operations and a relentless pursuit of justice, forged the agency's identity. Whether it was hunting down war criminals or rescuing hostages from the jaws of terrorism, Mossad's pursuit of a safer Israel was unwavering.

The agency's pivotal role in acquiring a MiG-21 fighter jet through Operation Diamond underscored its evolution into a significant player in the global intelligence community. The knowledge gained from this audacious mission gave Israel a decisive edge during the Six-Day War, demonstrating the far-reaching impact of Mossad's operations.

The legacy of Israeli intelligence, intricately interwoven with the nation's sense of security, found its ultimate expression in the aftermath of the Six-Day War. Israel's swift victory not only reshaped the geopolitical landscape but also amplified the myths and legends surrounding Israeli intelligence. It projected a newfound sense of self-security, even as Israel's neighbors plotted their revenge.

Yet, as the chapter's conclusion suggests, the Six-Day War also set the stage for the simmering tensions and enduring hostilities that would continue to shape the Middle East. Mossad's journey, marked by extraordinary successes and sobering challenges, mirrors Israel's complex and evolving role in this tumultuous region.

PART II

CHAPTER 10: SHIFTING TIDES

The Six-Day War

The Six-Day War of 1967 reshaped the geopolitical landscape of the Middle East, with Israel emerging as a dominant force in the region. Mossad, one of the world's most effective intelligence agencies, found itself at a pivotal juncture. Its mission remained unwavering: to prevent another Holocaust, ensuring the security and survival of the Jewish state. In the aftermath of the war, Israel's occupation of the West Bank, Gaza Strip, the Golan Heights, and the Sinai Peninsula presented both opportunities and challenges. These occupied territories served as bargaining chips in prospective peace negotiations with neighboring Arab countries, yet they also fueled simmering tensions.

Mossad's role expanded as it recognized the need to adapt to this new reality. The agency's ability to navigate the complex landscape of post-war politics would be tested. As the world's eyes turned to Jerusalem, Mossad delved deeper into the shadowy world of espionage and covert operations. It was in this charged atmosphere that Mossad licensed its agents to manipulate and, if necessary, eliminate threats. The controversial and high-stakes game of espionage played out on the world stage with significant impact.

One operation that sent shockwaves across the region was the assassination of a Hezbollah commander. Mossad's covert involvement in this bold act of retribution showcased its determination to protect Israeli interests. But Mossad's reach extended far beyond its immediate borders. The agency's fingerprints could be found in the most unlikely places, including the assassination of a leading Iranian nuclear scientist. Such operations had a profound impact on global politics, shaping alliances and conflicts.

For half a century, Mossad had been involved in every major incident in the region. Its influence and reputation were both feared and powerful. The agency's relentless pursuit of its mission had made it a dominant player on the world stage. As Mossad's operations continued to evolve, the shadow war it waged would impact the future of Israel and the entire Middle East. In this ever-shifting landscape, the agency's role remained pivotal. The story of Mossad was far from over; it was an enduring narrative of intrigue, power, and the pursuit of security in a region marked by conflict and complexity.

CHAPTER 11: THE RISE OF PALESTINIAN RESISTANCE

The aftermath of the Six-Day War presented Israel with a paradoxical situation. The occupation of the West Bank, Gaza Strip, Golan Heights, and Sinai Peninsula had bolstered Israeli territorial claims. However, it also sowed the seeds of a new conflict that had been festering for over two decades. The Palestinian territories, now under Israeli control, were at the heart of a growing challenge.

Israeli intelligence, including Mossad, faced the pressing need to adapt to this new reality. The Palestinian territories became a breeding ground for a potent mix of nationalistic fervor and radicalism. Within the refugee camps that housed dispossessed Palestinians, young people were increasingly willing to embrace more extreme ideologies. Mossad, at that time, did not fully comprehend the extent of this radicalization.

One of the notable figures of this era, who would later become the Palestinian representative in West Germany, was emblematic of a generation that grew up in the harsh conditions of Gaza's refugee camps. These young Palestinians were initially told by Arab countries that they would be helped to return home, but as time passed, they realized that this promise was empty. It was in these camps that a sense of self-reliance and resistance began to take root.

The cramped living conditions in the refugee camps forced Palestinians to get to know each other better. It was in these conditions that resistance movements began to form, setting the stage for what would become a significant challenge for Israeli intelligence.

Mossad and the entire Israeli intelligence community viewed the rise of Palestinian resistance as a formidable challenge. The territories under Israeli control offered the opportunity to recruit individuals who could be sent to carry out acts of terrorism, further exacerbating the security

CHAPTER 12: ARAFAT'S ASCENT

Mossad's Elusive Target

In the wake of the Six-Day War, Israel's decision to use force against the radical Palestinian factions inadvertently had the opposite effect. The Palestinians' newfound national consciousness began to crystallize, with various groups rallying around a common cause.

One prominent organization at the forefront of this resistance was the Palestine Liberation Organization (PLO), led by Yasser Arafat. The PLO was a leftist and secular movement, and its ranks were filled with fighters who were willing to take up arms for Palestinian self-determination. In the early years, Islam played a relatively minor role within the organization. Fatah, a faction within the PLO, aimed at nothing less than the complete liberation of Palestine, which, in their words, meant wiping Israel off the map.

Yasser Arafat, a former building contractor and co-founder of Fatah in 1957, assumed leadership of the PLO. Arafat was now Israel's prime enemy, a symbol of Palestinian resistance, and a prime target for Mossad. Israel's numerous attempts to assassinate Arafat only fueled his legend among his own people and around the world. Arafat survived these assassination attempts, often turning them into opportunities for political posturing.

He would hide from Israeli operatives in neighboring Arab countries and export PLO terrorism to other parts of the world. At that time, with open skies and open borders, there were limited capabilities for law enforcement to track and apprehend those involved in international terrorism.

As the Palestinian diaspora grew, so did the PLO's influence in Europe. Palestinian networks were established at universities and in working-class neighborhoods. Arafat's cause found sympathetic allies in the burgeoning left-wing student movements across the continent. The Palestinian struggle became a focal point for these students, and they actively supported and spread the Palestinian message.

Abdallah al-Franji, a student at the University of Frankfurt, recalls that the general sentiment in Europe was often in favor of the Palestinian cause. As demonstrations sprang up, students like him actively organized and participated. They distributed Palestinian scarves and echoed Palestinian slogans. The world was, indeed, a vast and interconnected place, and the PLO was quick to leverage this to its advantage.

The stage was set for a complex and far-reaching conflict. Mossad faced the daunting challenge of countering the PLO's activities on an international scale. Arafat, the elusive symbol of Palestinian resistance, remained a high-value target, but capturing or eliminating him would prove to be a formidable task that would stretch the limits of Israeli intelligence. The shadow war continued to evolve, with consequences that reverberated around the globe.

CHAPTER 13: MOSSAD'S BATTLE ON EUROPEAN SOIL

The Palestinian cause was resonating across the world, drawing support and sympathy, particularly among young Palestinians studying in Europe. Mossad's attention turned to this growing movement, recognizing the potential threats it posed. Abdallah al-Franji, a student at the University of Frankfurt, recalls that, at the time, support for the Palestinian cause was widespread, especially among students. The Palestinian diaspora was expanding, and with it, networks of activists were forming. They actively organized demonstrations, distributed Palestinian scarves, and amplified Palestinian slogans. No matter where they spoke, their message was well-received.

Mossad case officer Rafi Eitan received warnings from informants about the growing threats posed by Palestinian students in Germany. As the head of the European division, Eitan became increasingly concerned as he learned that students were being recruited into Fatah, with plans to create cells within the student community for potential terrorist attacks against Jews.

Frankfurt became a focal point for Mossad agents, especially a rented apartment used by the Palestinian students for their meetings. While the location was not particularly secretive, the discussions held there formed the basis for decision-making within the Palestinian student movement. Rafi Eitan decided to take action, suggesting that they intervene in the early stages of this growing threat. He ordered the apartment to be bugged, despite the absence of guards or significant security measures.

Mossad was becoming increasingly alarmed as the PLO carried out spectacular terrorist attacks, including dramatic skyjackings. These acts of terror were intended to draw global attention to the Palestinian cause, and they certainly achieved that goal, with images broadcast on TV screens worldwide. Mossad worked tirelessly to obtain information about planned attacks before they could be carried out. However, they found it challenging to rely on the cooperation of Europe's intelligence services. Israeli alerts to these European intelligence services and law enforcement often fell on deaf ears, as some European countries preferred to maintain an alleged neutrality in the Israeli-Palestinian conflict. As a result, they failed to take decisive action against known terrorists operating on their soil.

CHAPTER 14: MUNICH MASSACRE

Mossad's Toughest Challenge

In the early 1970s, Mossad's relentless battle against terrorism continued. Within Israel's borders, Mossad had the authority to arrest or eliminate militant Palestinians who posed threats. However, in Europe, the situation was far more complicated. The 1972 Olympic Games in Munich would become a harrowing episode in Mossad's history, testing the agency's capabilities and resolve on foreign soil.

West Germany had high hopes for the Munich Olympics, aiming to use the event to improve its global image. Policemen were deliberately unarmed, and the games were designed to be cheerful and cosmopolitan. However, the security experts in Germany had already warned that Israeli athletes were at risk when they competed internationally, and this danger was particularly heightened in Munich. Scenario drills had even been conducted, simulating potential attacks on the Olympic Village and Israeli athletes.

Despite the warnings and intelligence pointing to a potential assassination during the Olympics, Mossad lacked precise information about when and where the attack would occur. They only had a vague sense that something was amiss. In the world of intelligence, having vague information can be frustrating and, as events unfolded, tragic. The Munich Olympics turned into a catastrophe as Palestinian terrorists infiltrated the Olympic

Village on Tuesday morning. They killed two members of the Israeli Olympic team and took at least 13 hostages. The terrorists demanded the release of more than 200 of their comrades held in Israeli prisons and the release of two prominent German Red Army Faction terrorists.

Subsequent investigations would reveal that some of the Palestinian terrorists had studied in West Germany without ever arousing Mossad's suspicion. The terrorists issued an ultimatum, threatening to execute the hostages if their demands were not met. Israel's Prime Minister, Golda Meir, faced an agonizing decision. She ultimately rejected the terrorists' demands, setting the stage for a dramatic and deadly standoff that would mark one of Mossad's toughest challenges yet. The events in Munich would have far-reaching implications, not only for Mossad but for the entire world.

A Tragic Failure

Israel's Prime Minister, Golda Meir, faced a harrowing decision. Fearing the potential repercussions of capitulating to the terrorists' demands, she ultimately rejected their ultimatum. In her desperation to gain a better understanding of the situation, she dispatched the head of Mossad, Svi Samir, to Munich.

Upon arriving in Munich, Svi Samir found himself in a difficult position. The German authorities firmly refused to allow Israeli soldiers to intervene and free the hostages. Instead, inexperienced snipers in sweatsuits were deployed to observe the situation. The terrorists were aware of this, watching the unfolding events on television within the Olympic Village. As the planned rescue operation faltered, the terrorists seized the initiative. They demanded safe passage for themselves and the hostages aboard a plane bound for Cairo. The hostages, their hands and feet bound, walked past Samir, flanked by the terrorists. The silence was deafening.

The German crisis team reluctantly appeared to accept the terrorists' demands. Helicopters were provided to transport the group to a military airfield, with plans to storm the airfield before the terrorists could escape to Egypt. Samir was on the scene, lying beside a German sniper, watching helplessly as the tragic events unfolded. A Palestinian terrorist tossed a hand grenade into one of the helicopters, engulfing it in flames. This act resulted in the death of all the hostages in the first helicopter and five of the eight terrorists in a subsequent gunfight with the police. In the second helicopter, the Israeli hostages were shot and killed, and none of the athletes survived.

The Munich Massacre left 11 Israeli athletes dead, marking a horrifying tragedy that reverberated throughout Israel and the world. It was a momentous failure for both the Israeli government and Mossad, as they were unable to protect Jews on foreign soil.

A few weeks later, another grim chapter unfolded when a Palestinian terror commando hijacked a Lufthansa jet, demanding the release of the surviving hostage-takers from Munich. The German government controversially complied with their demands, releasing the assassins who were subsequently celebrated as heroes in the Arab world. It was a bitter and painful moment for Israel, a stark reminder of the challenges it faced in combating terrorism and protecting its citizens abroad.

CHAPTER 15: CRUSADE AGAINST TERROR

Mossad's Retaliation

In the aftermath of the Munich Massacre, a devastating blow to Israel and its people, the Jewish state found itself in a precarious position. The German government's decision to release the surviving Palestinian hostage-takers was seen as a grave injustice. Prime Minister Golda Meir, under immense pressure and with elections on the horizon, made a momentous decision. She gave Mossad the green light for an unprecedented crusade against terrorism. If the battlefield was shifting to Europe, then Mossad would follow, not just to thwart impending attacks but to dismantle the very networks that orchestrated them.

The Israeli cabinet granted Mossad the authority to eliminate Palestinian operatives in Europe, even if it meant blatantly violating international rules and laws. The reasoning behind this decision was clear: Israel had to act decisively to protect its citizens when no one else would. Mossad, traditionally an agency focused on intelligence gathering and reconnaissance, had to evolve. They now required operatives with a different skill set, individuals who could track down and eliminate the masterminds behind terrorist activities. A special task force called "Caesarea" was formed for precisely this purpose, embodying the public image of Mossad for decades to come.

The inner structure of Mossad remained shrouded in secrecy, but the agency's eight central departments were known to those in the intelligence community. Among them, Caesarea, responsible for covert operations and assassinations, took on the challenging task of eliminating those who posed a threat to Israel. Tav, another department, focused on cooperation with allied secret services, gathering intelligence through wiretapping, surveillance, and even burglaries. Summit, the largest department, was tasked with collecting information from human sources and maintaining a global network of informants.

Mossad's campaign against Palestinian terrorists in Europe began in October 1972, driven by a desire for revenge and the need to prevent further acts of terror. To achieve this, Mossad needed to take measures that terrorists could not predict or counter. The agency's assassinations were carried out covertly but with the intent of sending a clear message to potential threats. Mossad's commandos, adept at moving unnoticed, made their presence felt across Western Europe, signifying the agency's commitment to defending Israel and its people.

The retaliatory actions of Mossad would cast a long shadow, as the agency embarked on a relentless mission to protect Israel and its interests, no matter where in the world the threat emerged.

CHAPTER 16: MOSSAD'S COVERT PURSUIT IN EUROPE

Mossad's relentless pursuit of Palestinian terrorists in Europe demanded a level of cunning and secrecy that left their enemies perplexed. It was crucial to operate in a manner that left no room for questions, to ensure that no one could ask, "What are you doing here?"

Mossad's assassinations were conducted in the shadows, yet they bore a visible message to terrorists in Western Europe – a stark warning that Israel would not tolerate threats to its security. The agency's commandos, skilled in the art of discretion, moved freely and without hesitation. In case of capture, the consequence was often a prison sentence, a risk they willingly embraced to protect their homeland.

While the majority of their operations went unnoticed, the most significant targets found refuge in Arab countries, making them considerably harder to reach. Take, for instance, Abdallah al-Franji, the former spokesman for Palestinian students in West Germany. His close ties to the assassins from Munich led to his arrest by German authorities. Remarkably, being in jail saved his life, for Mossad had him marked as a target.

Franji's comrades were no longer safe in Germany, and the Germans were eager to rid themselves of PLO members. They went to great lengths to fabricate evidence against him, eventually expelling him from the country. Al-Franji found asylum in Algeria, a relatively safer place to continue his work for the PLO.

Returning to Europe was simply too perilous. Mossad's reach was extensive, and their pursuit was unrelenting. Al-Franji's position as the PLO's European representative led him to run the organization's office from Algeria, alongside a comrade.

In one harrowing incident, a thick envelope held by his friend exploded when opened. The explosion threw al-Franji across the room and left his friend severely injured. Despite the close call, al-Franji survived, a testament to the dangers he faced in his role.

Mossad's history is replete with both successes and failures, and one operation in Lillehammer, Norway, stands out as an epic failure. It was a disastrous mix-up that resulted in the mistaken killing of a Moroccan waiter, believed to be Ali Hassan Salameh, the alleged mastermind of the Munich attack. To make matters worse, the Israeli agents involved were apprehended by the Norwegian police. The trial and subsequent revelations about Mossad's methods had far-reaching consequences, exposing communication channels and agent hideouts, damaging the Secret Service's reputation across Europe.

This marked a temporary end to the vendetta against the PLO in Europe. Yasir Arafat and Abu Jihad decided to reduce most of their operations in Europe. Terrorist attacks in Western countries were tarnishing their image. However, not everyone adhered to this directive, and some factions continued to carry out assaults and hostage takings.

In 1979, Mossad succeeded in eliminating a top terrorist using a car bomb, someone they had been pursuing for quite a while. Their intended target in Lillehammer, Ali Hassan Salameh, was finally brought to justice.

CHAPTER 17:
EXPANDING REACH

Africa and the Power of Alliances

Mossad's influence extended well beyond Europe. They received requests for assistance from various corners of the globe, earning a reputation as the "Superman" of espionage. Mossad's involvement extended to unexpected regions, with a notable operation that changed the course of African history.

Mossad had been assisting Christian rebels in southern Sudan since 1969. These rebels were fighting against the oppression of the predominantly Arab central government and saw Israel as a natural ally. One of the three agents sent by Mossad was David Ben Uziel, a doctor involved in a mission aimed at making life difficult for the northern Sudanese Army. Their mission included forming a 1,000-man battalion, establishing a landing strip, creating medics and signaling courses, and providing arms to the rebels.

In a remarkable endeavor, Mossad operatives find themselves in the primeval forests of southern Sudan, far from Israel's borders. Their mission: to establish a formidable rebel army capable of challenging the Sudanese government's troops. But why would Mossad venture so far from home?

The answer lies in geopolitics. Egypt and Sudan are prime concerns for Israel. Egypt's potential plans to reclaim the Sinai Peninsula, lost during the Six-Day War, had Israel on high alert. Mossad's strategy was clear: by supporting the southern Sudanese rebels in their struggle against the Sudanese government, they aimed to keep Sudan occupied with internal conflict, making it less likely to join forces with Egypt against Israel.

This operation wasn't an act of charity. Mossad, like intelligence agencies worldwide, acted in its own interests. In the complex world of espionage, the principle of "my enemy's enemy is my friend" reigns supreme. Israel sought allies in Africa to weaken its adversaries. Africa held significant importance because it presented a unique opportunity to break the ring of hostile Arab countries surrounding Israel.

Mossad undertook missions in Africa under foreign identities, operating with a clear political agenda. The goal was to strengthen minority groups in the Middle East and Arab countries, forging alliances with the Kurds in Iraq and Christians in Lebanon. Israel aimed to empower these minorities, creating potential allies in a region otherwise marked by hostility.

The connections made in Africa were seen as valuable assets in the fight against Palestinian terrorism. Israel's diplomatic, intelligence, and covert outreach efforts had far-reaching consequences in shaping alliances and influencing events on the African continent.

Operation Entebbe - A Daring Rescue

The stage is set in Uganda, a country led by the unpredictable dictator, Idi Amin. An Air France jet carrying mainly Israeli passengers is hijacked and rerouted to Uganda. Responsibility for this audacious act is claimed by a radical PLO splinter group under the leadership of Wadi Haddad, a mastermind of several previous skyjackings. Surprisingly, Idi Amin, who once had ties to Mossad, accommodates the hostage-takers.

However, Israel, well-informed about the airport facilities, plans a daring mission to free the hostages. The airport had been constructed by an Israeli company, providing Mossad with access to the original blueprints. Mossad agents gather recent information, with one posing as an amateur pilot and taking aerial photographs of the airport. They even secure a private plane from neighboring Kenya, a country with strong connections to Mossad. Mossad's intelligence proves crucial, and a team of commandos, camouflaged as a commercial aircraft, is flown to Entebbe for a daring rescue operation.

This operation aligns with the Periphery Doctrine, allowing Israel to intervene in the heart of Africa and the hinterland of the southern Arab world. More than 100 hostages are successfully rescued in the operation, defying any notion of negotiations with terrorists. The mission's success is a prestigious triumph for Mossad and serves as a clear example of Israel's resolve in the face of terrorism.

Yet, while Mossad shines in this operation, its history is not without moments of overconfidence and oversight. In Egypt, President Anwar Sadat's threats to reclaim the Sinai Peninsula are underestimated by Israel and its intelligence services, including Mossad. They disregard Sadat's public warnings, relying on the service to provide early alerts, as Mossad has an informant within the Egyptian government, codenamed "Angel." However, complacency and underestimation will prove to be grave mistakes as events unfold in the region.

◆ ◆ ◆

CHAPTER 18: THE YOM KIPPUR WAR

The Warning Unheeded

In the autumn of 1973, the Middle East was fraught with tension. Israel's intelligence community had its eyes on Egyptian and Syrian troop movements along the borders. However, these activities were perceived as routine maneuvers. After all, they believed that if an Arab attack were imminent, Ashraf Marwan, their prized informant within the Egyptian government, would have provided ample warning.

Ashraf Marwan, codenamed "Angel," was one of President Anwar Sadat's most trusted advisors. But he had a complex motivation for spying for Mossad. Some speculate it was driven by a desire for revenge against Sadat, who had married his daughter for political gain rather than affection. Others believe that financial motives played a part in his decision.

The tipping point came when Ashraf Marwan invited Mossad to London and issued a stark warning: war was imminent. He stressed the urgency of the situation. This message was disconcerting, given that Marwan had previously provided intelligence that had not materialized into action. Mossad Director Zvi Zamir, in consultation with his team, faced a critical decision.

Zamir's hesitation was fueled by the fear of making a false alarm. If he alerted the Prime Minister, the Minister of Defense, and the

Chief of Staff, only for the predicted war not to materialize, it would have severe consequences for his career and the Mossad's credibility.

However, Mossad chose to heed the warning of their top spy within the Egyptian government. According to Marwan, the invasion was set to occur on Yom Kippur, a holy day. Despite lingering doubts, Mossad made the fateful call to alert Israel's leadership, marking a pivotal moment in the events to come.

The Fallout and Shift in Foreign Policy

The Yom Kippur War, which erupted on the holiest day in the Jewish calendar, was a devastating wake-up call for Israel. On this day of rest and fasting, public life in Israel traditionally stood still. Rushing people out of synagogues on a false alarm could have been fatal. The situation demanded careful consideration.

In the midst of the crisis, a five-line telegram was composed. It conveyed a dire message: war would break out. The message left no address and stated, "I'm unavailable; this is my message to you, you decide." Israel's military, however, hesitated. The armed forces did not mobilize until a mere 14 hours before the outbreak of war. This delay would exact a heavy toll.

Israel would ultimately emerge victorious in this conflict as well, but not without significant losses for a small nation. Ashraf Marwan's warning had been heeded at the eleventh hour, but the price was high, paid in blood.

Ashraf Marwan continued to work for Mossad from his London residence, a shadowy figure providing valuable intelligence. However, it wasn't until 2002, three decades after the Yom Kippur War, that his identity was exposed. This revelation marked one of the worst Israeli intelligence failures, tarnishing the reputation of

Mossad and Israel's ability to protect its assets.

The question of whether Marwan might have been a double agent lingers, compounded by the mysteries surrounding his death in 2007 when he fell from the balcony of his London apartment. Despite these uncertainties, one thing remains clear: Marwan, code named "Angel," had saved countless Israeli lives.

The Yom Kippur War not only shook the image of Israel's intelligence services but also eroded trust in Israeli politics. Policymakers began to doubt the intelligence they received, leading to a fundamental shift in foreign policy. Israeli leaders such as Perez and Rabin increasingly relied on their own assessments, independent of the intelligence agencies.

The war shattered the belief in Israel's military invincibility, prompting a need for covert diplomacy. Mossad had already been discreetly building contacts in the region, laying the foundation for a new era in Israeli foreign policy.

CHAPTER 19: COVERT DIPLOMACY AND THE HISTORIC PEACE NEGOTIATIONS

In the aftermath of the Yom Kippur War and the realization that the region's political dynamics had shifted, Mossad recognized the need for a new approach. The agency extended its reach beyond covert operations and espionage, delving into the world of secret and clandestine diplomacy. Reuven Shiloah, the first head of Mossad, played a pivotal role in this evolution.

Shiloah's vision was clear: establishing secret channels of diplomacy would serve as a temporary solution until the official diplomatic landscape could thaw from the deep freeze it was in. These secret endeavors would allow Israel to discreetly build contacts in the region, fostering relations with both opposition groups and government officials in various Middle Eastern countries.

Mossad's influence extended to nations such as Turkey, Iran, and Ethiopia, which also viewed the Arab nations as potential threats. In particular, Iran played a crucial role in the covert collaboration with Israel, given its regional positioning.

Even some Arab states, such as Oman and Morocco, maintained clandestine ties to Tel Aviv. King Hassan II of Morocco, a pro-Western monarch, recognized the value of Israel's intelligence capabilities and turned to Mossad for assistance in monitoring internal opposition.

This cooperation paid off in 1977 when Israel's foreign minister, Moshe Dayan, secretly traveled to Morocco. During his visit, Dayan indicated that Israel might consider withdrawing from the Sinai Peninsula, a statement that was made publicly in Parliament. It was an historic moment, signaling a willingness to engage in diplomacy.

Shortly thereafter, Anwar Sadat, the President of Egypt, expressed his desire to visit Jerusalem and negotiate with the Israelis. Mossad's secret preparations and Egypt's efforts to distance itself from Soviet influence created the conditions for this unprecedented move. Sadat viewed the peace negotiations not only as an opportunity to make peace with Israel but, more importantly, as a means to achieve peace within the region.

This significant turn of events led to the first-ever meeting between the heads of state of Israel and an Arab country. The peace negotiations with Egypt marked a revolutionary step, considering that, until the mid-1970s, Egypt had been one of Israel's staunchest adversaries. It was a historic moment when leaders from both nations sat down together to negotiate a peace treaty.

President Jimmy Carter of the United States played a pivotal role in hosting the tough negotiations between Israel and Egypt. The Camp David conference, often associated with the peace treaty, was a significant diplomatic effort, though it should perhaps be named the "Jimmy Carter conference" considering his relentless commitment to achieving a comprehensive agreement for the entire Middle East.

Carter's vision extended to fostering peace between all Middle

Eastern countries. However, it was Egypt and Israel that came to a decisive agreement, solidifying their political and strategic ties. Mossad had woven this intricate web of diplomatic maneuvering without direct American involvement, a testament to the agency's effectiveness in secret diplomacy.

CHAPTER 20: THE SHIFTING SANDS OF ALLIANCES

The peace treaty between Israel and Egypt sent shockwaves throughout the Arab world. Sadat faced expulsion from the Arab League and was assassinated three years later. Yet Israel continued to rely on Mossad's secret channels, recognizing that the head of intelligence often held the ruler's confidence in Arab and Muslim countries. Establishing secret communication with these intelligence heads allowed Israel to have a backdoor to the rulers. Israel's allure to potential partners included economic strength, diplomatic connections with the West, and access to top-secret information, which was of particular interest to dictators.

One example of such a partnership was with Iran, a covert ally since the 1950s. Under the rule of Mohammad Reza Shah Pahlavi, Iran leaned strongly towards the West. Despite its high oil revenues and deficit of human rights, Mossad collaborated closely with the Iranians. They established a strategic relationship, with Israel selling Iran oil and various other commodities. The Iranians, in turn, sought Israel's expertise in internal security— a mutually beneficial exchange that emphasized the complex web of regional alliances orchestrated by Mossad.

As Mossad's secret alliances continued to evolve, one of its notable covert partners was Iran. Since the 1950s, the agency had established a strategic relationship with the Iranian monarchy under Mohammad Reza Shah Pahlavi. Iran, with its strong pro-Western stance, became a crucial partner for Israel, thanks to its high oil revenues and alignment with Western powers.

Despite human rights concerns, Mossad's collaboration with Iran extended to various areas of mutual interest.

Israel provided Iran with oil and a range of commodities, while Iran sought Mossad's expertise in internal security. The latter included training and support, particularly in dealing with social tensions and potential unrest within Iran. This partnership emphasized Mossad's knack for building covert relationships driven by shared interests and realpolitik.

However, by 1978, the situation in Iran was rapidly deteriorating. Serious protests against the Shah's regime and economic disparities were mounting. The Shah appealed directly to Mossad, seeking the elimination of the exiled Islamic cleric Ayatollah Ruhollah Khomeini, who was inciting protests against the Shah's regime from abroad. This posed a moral and strategic dilemma for Mossad.

The Director of Mossad questioned the potential outcomes: If they succeeded in eliminating Khomeini, how would it affect international relations? If they failed, what would be the consequences? The decision was crucial and challenging, with ramifications on multiple fronts.

As the situation in Iran deteriorated further, a revolution broke out. Armed revolutionaries surrounded Mossad's headquarters, signaling the dire state of affairs in Iran. Mohammad Reza Shah Pahlavi eventually left the country, leading to the collapse of his regime.

Mossad's long standing partnership with Iran was irrevocably damaged as Khomeini returned to Iran and established an Islamic theocracy. The agency had to adapt to this new reality, with Iran becoming a mortal enemy that openly called for the annihilation of Israel.

In the wake of these changes, other actors saw opportunities in the Islamic revolution in Iran. Yasir Arafat and the Palestinian Liberation Organization (PLO) extended their hand to the new regime in Tehran. Palestinian nationalists and Iranian Islamists found common ground in their shared enmity toward the United States and Israel. Mossad was confronted with a new challenge —adversaries driven by religious fervor and a willingness to sacrifice their lives for their cause.

The era of Islamist extremism had dawned, adding another layer of complexity to the already intricate web of Middle Eastern alliances and rivalries. Mossad, as always, had to adapt to this shifting landscape while continuing its mission to safeguard Israel's interests.

PART III

CHAPTER 21: AGE OF ISLAMIST TERROR

The Deliberate Provocation

The early 1980s marked a period of escalating tension along Israel's northern border as Palestinian assassins, operating from refugee camps in southern Lebanon, continuously infiltrated Israeli territory. Mossad faced the immense challenge of locating and neutralizing these top-tier terrorists, whose operations were deeply entrenched within the camps.

Lebanon had evolved into a complex battlefield in the ongoing struggle against terrorism. After the expulsion of the PLO from Jordan in 1970, they had established their headquarters in Lebanon. Thousands of Palestinian refugees had been residing in camps in Lebanon since the founding of Israel, and over time, these camps had transformed into bases for terrorist activities, particularly in the southern region. Israeli military strikes aimed at these bases had failed to effectively eliminate the problem and often incited further acts of terrorism. Not even a ceasefire agreement with the PLO could bring a lasting end to the violence.

The situation had escalated to the point where radical forces were now setting the agenda, ignoring the PLO's official policies. The Israeli government, under the leadership of Prime Minister Menachem Begin, who had once carried out daring operations for Israel's independence, was determined to counter the terrorism emerging from its northern border. Begin found a kindred spirit in Ariel Sharon, who had been the defense minister since 1981.

In the face of these growing threats, Israel could not simply invade a foreign country to address the issue. Instead, the Israeli leadership adopted a strategic policy of deliberate provocation. By intentionally escalating the situation, Israel aimed to create the circumstances that would justify a military intervention.

As the tension grew in this volatile region, Mossad was confronted with a challenging task. This chapter delves into Mossad's pivotal role in navigating the complexities of combating terrorism along Israel's northern border, where covert operations played a critical role.

Mossad's unwavering commitment to protecting Israel and preventing another Holocaust led to a series of covert activities that would impact global politics through dramatic and, at times, controversial operations. In this volatile environment, the agency's ability to operate effectively was continually put to the test.

Prime Minister Begin and Defense Minister Sharon were determined to find a pretext for invading Lebanon, with the ultimate goal of expelling the PLO. Their belief was that by removing the PLO as a symbol of Palestinian nationalism, Israel would gain greater freedom of action in the West Bank.

However, the situation in Lebanon was far from simple. Various religious groups were vying for power, with substantial support from foreign entities. Israel backed the Christian militia, Iran supported the Shiites, and Syria intervened alongside the PLO. A bloody civil war had been raging in Lebanon since 1975.

In this tumultuous landscape, Mossad maintained close contact with Lebanon's Christian groups, as they saw the Palestinians as a mutual enemy. The Christian militias had been fighting against the PLO in a brutal civil war, and the situation resembled the Wild West, with violence and chaos.

While there were doubts about the reliability of the Christian militias, supporting them appeared to be the most viable means of influencing events in Lebanon. Mossad's involvement was discreet, and it avoided direct military intervention, such as an Israeli army incursion into Lebanon or the occupation of Beirut.

Operation Peace for Galilee

As the clock struck 10:53, Israeli armored units rolled into Lebanon, marking the beginning of a military operation that had the potential to reshape the turbulent region. The decision to deploy these forces came 50 minutes prior, setting into motion a complex and unpredictable series of events.

Israel's initial approach did not involve a direct invasion of Lebanon or a plan to occupy Beirut. Mossad had advised against a full-scale Israeli intervention in the Lebanese Civil War, given the intricacies and complications of the situation. However, Defense Minister Ariel Sharon had grand ambitions.

While the public discourse primarily focused on attacking PLO bases along the border, the true objective was to dismantle the PLO's infrastructure across Lebanon and expel Syrian forces from the region. Subsequently, the plan called for the installation of a pro-Israeli regime.

Approximately two months after the invasion began, the PLO surprisingly decided to retreat from Lebanon, marking a significant turning point. The strategy outlined by Ariel Sharon appeared to yield success. The leader of the Christian militias, Bashir Gemayel, became Lebanon's new president. Gemayel had extensive connections with Israel, fueling hope for a pro-Israeli administration in Lebanon.

However, tragedy struck when Bashir Gemayel was assassinated in September 1982, likely in a bomb attack carried out by Syria's Secret Service. The aftermath of his assassination unleashed a wave of anger and a thirst for revenge among his followers.

At Mossad headquarters, the atmosphere was tense as they monitored the situation closely. Members of Mossad's political department and Christian militia representatives were present. The Christian militia, driven by a thirst for vengeance, targeted two Palestinian refugee camps, resulting in the brutal murder of several hundred innocent civilians.

Despite their objectives, Mossad had overestimated the influence of the Christian militias and their ability to maintain power. Israel's intervention failed to quell the fires of civil conflict in Lebanon; rather, it inadvertently stoked the flames of violence.

A critical factor in this failure was the failure to grasp the demographic shifts within Lebanon, which had reshaped the balance of power among different religious and ethnic communities. The consequences of this oversight led to Israel being drawn deeper into the quagmire of Lebanese internal conflicts. The Lebanese Civil War continued unabated, defying Israel's initial expectations.

CHAPTER 22: THE ETHIOPIAN EXODUS

As the aftermath of the failed Lebanon operation cast a shadow over Israeli politics, Minister Ariel Sharon and Prime Minister Menachem Begin faced mounting pressure, ultimately leading to their resignations. Mossad found itself at the center of criticism, despite the fact that its experts had originally discouraged a full-scale invasion. The intelligence community was held responsible for misjudging the complex situation in Lebanon.

In the corridors of power, the political imperatives of Israeli leaders often took precedence over the warnings and assessments of intelligence services. The pressure on political leaders to take forceful action, especially in the face of a perceived threat, is a familiar scenario not only in Israel but also in other countries. One notable example is the 2003 Iraq War, which followed the 9/11 terrorist attacks and involved the politicization and selective use of intelligence.

The question of whether a Mossad director can significantly influence a prime minister's decisions in strategic geopolitical matters remains a contentious one. Prime ministers must navigate a broad spectrum of factors, including their personal ideology, political maneuvering, and the imperative of maintaining their political longevity. In such contexts, intelligence agencies like Mossad may act as service providers, offering information and analysis, but their influence on political decisions may be limited.

Mossad's real power and influence are demonstrated in a different theater of operations: East Africa. In Ethiopia, a Jewish community with roots dating back to Biblical times has faced increasing risks in the early 1980s. Tens of thousands of Ethiopian Jews are in danger, both from violence and hunger.

The Israeli government, under the leadership of Prime Minister Menachem Begin, decided to bring the Ethiopian Jews to Israel. However, this operation had to be executed in utmost secrecy. Mossad was entrusted with the mission to rescue these vulnerable Jewish communities who had been living in Ethiopia and who had fled to refugee camps in neighboring Sudan.

Operation Diving Paradise

Jaafar al-Nimeiry, the dictator of Sudan, is a formidable obstacle in Mossad's mission to rescue Ethiopian Jews. While Israeli intelligence is primarily tasked with ensuring the safety of Israel, it takes on an extraordinary responsibility — safeguarding Jews worldwide, even if they are not Israeli citizens. This unique aspect of Mossad's mandate sets it apart from other intelligence organizations and underscores the profound commitment to Jewish communities around the world.

Rescue operations have been a fundamental part of Mossad's history. In its early years, Israel conducted dramatic operations, bringing hundreds of thousands of Jewish immigrants to the newly formed nation, effectively doubling its population. After World War II, European Jews were covertly smuggled into Palestine, laying the foundation for the State of Israel. Over time, Mossad focused on the extraction of Jewish communities from Arab countries, facilitating their return to the land of their ancestors.

Fast forward 30 years, and Mossad faces an extraordinary challenge: how to bring the Ethiopian Jews to Israel. This operation defied conventional wisdom, breaking every rule in the clandestine operation handbook. The complexity of the mission was compounded by the limited reconnaissance capabilities in the region, making it virtually impossible to ensure the agents' safety and maintain their cover.

A seemingly ordinary holiday resort on the Sudanese coast becomes the covert launchpad for the audacious rescue mission. Mossad agents, posing as European and American resort staff, live undetected in Sudan for years, all while managing the diving resort. These individuals were not given the luxury of extensive training, but the urgency of the mission demanded a shortcut. Crash courses were administered to prepare them for operating under assumed identities in a hostile and unfamiliar environment.

As Mossad agents posed as European and American resort staff, their lives were a delicate dance on the edge of discovery. They operated undetected in Sudan for years, with the everyday routine of managing the diving resort. During the daytime, they attended to the needs of the resort's guests, seamlessly blending in. But their true mission came to life under the cloak of night, when they smuggled Jews out of the country.

Gad Shimron, a co-founder and manager of the resort, took on a dual role as both journalist and Mossad agent. He posed as a windsurfing instructor and boat operator, even introducing windsurfing to Sudan by flying in the first board from Israel aboard a military plane. Over time, their cover at the Diving Paradise became second nature, allowing them to maintain their facade while executing the covert operation.

The agents struck a balance between maintaining a casual relationship with the tourists and managing the intricate operations of the resort. However, there were moments when their cover teetered on the brink, and a single slip could endanger their lives. The knowledge that a simple mistake could jeopardize the entire operation weighed heavily on them. While they partied and danced with the guests one night, they knew that, behind the resort's facade, a convoy of trucks was transporting Jews to an evacuation point.

The extraction of Ethiopian Jews from Sudan involved two primary methods: transporting them across the Red Sea by boat and secretly flying out larger groups. The latter became necessary as conditions in the refugee camps deteriorated. These nighttime operations were fraught with danger, the very essence of risk.

During one mission, the agents stumbled into a Sudanese Army ambush, suddenly confronted by about 60 Sudanese soldiers armed with AK-47s. In an extraordinary display of quick thinking and audacity, Danny, one of the Mossad agents, raised his hands in surrender and berated the officer, branding him an idiot for opening fire on innocent tourists. This audacious move not only saved their lives but left the Sudanese soldiers embarrassed and apologizing, swiftly leaving the scene.

Other clashes with Sudanese soldiers occurred, but Mossad's resourcefulness ensured the successful continuation of the transports. Part of this ingenuity involved substantial bribes to the ruling dictator, a discreet exchange that allowed Sudan to save face in the Arab world.

Every group of Jews successfully transported from the Sudanese shore by naval commandos and aboard planes carried with it a sense of hope and triumph. Mossad's audacious Operation Diving

Paradise continued to write a remarkable chapter in the history of rescue operations, demonstrating the lengths they would go to bring Jewish communities to safety and freedom.

The Unseen Heroes of Mossad

Mossad's clandestine operations to rescue Ethiopian Jews were more than just daring feats of espionage; they were a testament to the unwavering dedication of its agents. While discreetly extracting Jewish communities from hostile territory, Mossad agents were not driven by immorality or violence but by a profound sense of purpose and humanity.

In their mission, Mossad agents had to tread lightly, often concealing their true identities. Unlike the fictionalized James Bond archetype with flashy weaponry, the most dangerous weapon for a Mossad agent would be to get caught in possession of arms in a foreign land where they were not meant to be. In such operations, their identity and cover story were their only defense against discovery.

One of the significant challenges faced by these agents was the need to hide their Jewish identity, as exposure could lead to dire consequences in enemy territory. Despite the enormous personal risks, Mossad had no difficulty recruiting agents. In fact, its budget had expanded over the years, and its manpower continued to grow. The recent demand for cyber experts has also become a focal point for recruitment.

However, the selection process for Mossad agents was meticulous. They were not looking for individuals who simply fit the mold of a spy; they sought a unique combination of qualities. Agents had to be trustworthy and morally upright individuals. Still, they also needed the capacity to transform into entirely different personas when the situation demanded it. This blend of unwavering integrity and adaptability was rare, making successful recruits stand out like diamonds in the rough.

The career prospects for those who possessed these traits were promising. The close connections between the security sector and politics in Israel provided an excellent platform for advancement. Once you joined, you were part of a tightly-knit group – a boys and girls club where gender played no role in defining capability. These elite operatives demonstrated that being a Mossad agent required not only physical courage but also the moral fiber to navigate a world filled with ethical challenges, secrecy, and transformation.

These unseen heroes of Mossad embarked on their missions, often in the shadows, driven by a profound commitment to their cause and an unshakable sense of duty, demonstrating that in the world of intelligence, courage and integrity are the ultimate tools of power.

CHAPTER 23: THE OSLO ACCORDS

The Intifada and New Threats

As the 1980s unfolded, Mossad was facing shifting challenges in the ever-turbulent Middle East. The tranquil shores of Sudan that had served as the backdrop for the daring Ethiopian rescue operation became a memory, as a military coup in 1985 abruptly halted Mossad's presence in the country. The new leaders publicly denounced their predecessor, Jaafar al-Nimeiry, as a collaborator and a sympathizer of Jews, forcing the Israeli agents to abandon the coastal resort where they had successfully operated for nearly a decade. Tragically, during those years, nearly 4,000 Ethiopian Jews lost their lives before Mossad could reach them. Still, the operation, on the whole, stood as a significant success for Mossad, bringing around 20,000 Ethiopian Jews to safety in Israel by 1985.

However, the challenges didn't end with the successful rescue. Integrating this new wave of African Jews into Israeli society proved to be another complex task, raising questions about cultural assimilation and identity.

In 1987, a new storm was brewing in Gaza, an area under Israeli occupation for more than two decades. The Palestinian population, particularly the youth, was growing increasingly frustrated due to a lack of opportunities and a bleak future. This discontent served as fertile ground for the birth of a new wave of violence, the First Intifada. Mossad, historically focused on combating the PLO, was caught off guard by this uprising as it was an internal Palestinian struggle. The agents, accustomed to operating on foreign soil where Palestinian leaders found refuge, had to navigate this new domestic challenge.

The Intifada marked a turning point. Mossad had traditionally considered the PLO, based in faraway Tunis, as the primary source of Palestinian threats. However, the agents soon realized that the real power resided within the occupied territories, closer to home.

In this ever-changing landscape, Mossad had to adapt to the new reality, where the enemy was not on a distant battleground but within Israel's own borders. The challenges would only intensify in the years to come as Mossad faced a new breed of adversaries, armed with religious fervor and an unwavering determination to defy Israel.

The conflict intensified, leading to a search for a diplomatic solution. Israelis and Palestinians, after years of violence, finally sat down for talks in Oslo, Norway. The negotiations offered a glimpse of hope for a lasting peace, and Israel's Prime Minister Yitzhak Rabin was cautiously optimistic. However, Rabin was wary of involving the intelligence services, preferring to approach the negotiations with a more diplomatic perspective. This decision, driven by his Foreign Minister Shimon Peres, aimed to avoid the pitfalls of viewing the conflict through the lens of covert operations.

Mossad's role in the peace process had always been significant, as evidenced by its involvement in the Egypt-Israel peace treaty. However, under Rabin's leadership, the intelligence chiefs found themselves relegated to the shadows. They were accustomed to operating in the covert realm, but now, the diplomatic stage was shifting, and their involvement was diminishing.

As the Oslo Accords took shape, there was a growing sense

of anticipation, both in Israel and on the international stage. Yet, beneath the facade of diplomacy, shadows of intrigue and uncertainty persisted. Mossad's transition from covert operator to diplomatic observer presented its own set of challenges, leaving the intelligence agency in a state of ambiguity as the tides of peace and diplomacy ebbed and flowed.

"Mossad's leadership considered itself not just an intelligence agency but also a key player in diplomatic efforts. Their involvement in the peace treaty with Egypt had solidified their role on the international stage. However, their diplomatic ambitions sometimes clashed with the priorities of their political leaders.

In the early 1990s, while peace talks were underway in Oslo, Norway, between Israel and the Palestine Liberation Organization (PLO), the Mossad was not as involved as it had been in previous diplomatic endeavors. The Mossad chiefs were aware of ongoing negotiations, but there was a distinct shift in their involvement.

Prime Minister Yitzhak Rabin, at the forefront of the Oslo Accords, seemed to downplay the Mossad's role. When the Mossad chiefs approached him, expressing concern about events unfolding in Europe, Rabin responded with a curt dismissal, saying, 'Drop it; I'm aware of it.'

This marked a departure from the previous close collaboration between Mossad and political leadership. Rabin's stance reflected the belief that intelligence agencies may not always offer relevant insights into complex diplomatic matters. He and his Foreign Minister, Shimon Peres, shared the view that intelligence services might not have been privy to key events like Munich and Pearl Harbor and, therefore, were not indispensable for their decision-making.

The Oslo peace talks resulted in the historic signing of a peace treaty in Washington in 1993. Yitzhak Rabin and Yasser Arafat received the Nobel Peace Prize the following year for their efforts. As part of the agreement, Israeli troops withdrew from the Gaza Strip and the West Bank, paving the way for Palestinian self-government in these territories.

However, the peace was not absolute. Some critical issues, such as the status of Israeli settlements and the future of Jerusalem, remained unresolved. Moreover, the peace process faced a new challenge. The Palestinian Liberation Organization (PLO) under Yasser Arafat, which had once represented all Palestinians, no longer spoke for the entirety of the Palestinian population.

Hamas, an Islamic terrorist organization led by Sheikh Ahmad Yasin, had gained considerable strength. Hamas aimed for a theocratic state and the destruction of Israel. Sheikh Yasin had founded Hamas during the First Intifada in 1987. He was even sentenced to life in prison by an Israeli court, but this only seemed to embolden the organization further.

Israel expected the PLO, under Arafat's leadership, to address the issue of Hamas and put an end to its terrorist activities. But the operations carried out by the Israeli intelligence community could potentially jeopardize the fragile peace process, leading to complex and challenging diplomatic and security situations."

Israel's approach at the time was that Hamas was indeed a problem, but as long as the Palestinian Authority, led by Arafat, wanted to continue the peace process, they would handle the issue. This approach assumed that the Palestinian leadership had the interest and ability to contain the rise of Hamas.

Unfortunately, this strategy faltered when the Palestinian

leadership, at a certain point, decided to slow down its efforts against Hamas. This marked the beginning of significant troubles. Hamas was no longer under control, and their actions grew increasingly audacious.

Hamas employed a deadly tactic that would shock Israel and the world: suicide bombings. These ruthless attacks targeted Israeli cities, and the victims included men, women, and even small children. As the new Prime Minister of Israel, Benjamin Netanyahu, took office in 1996, he faced an alarming wave of suicide bombings and an urgent need to address this evolving threat.

Prime Minister Netanyahu had a solemn responsibility to protect his citizens from this terrorist evil. However, countering Hamas, with its suicide bombings and its radical ideology, presented a unique challenge for the Israeli intelligence community.

The Prime Minister sought to identify potential targets within Hamas's leadership that could be neutralized to halt the devastating suicide attacks. This endeavor required comprehensive intelligence and precision. Mossad, Israel's renowned intelligence agency, undertook the daunting task of gathering intricate details about Hamas leaders – where they resided, their daily routines, and their associations.

However, there were additional complications. Many of the key Hamas leaders were based in Amman, Jordan, and they were heavily guarded. Mossad needed to penetrate this fortress of security to carry out any actions against these individuals. These operations demanded a level of precision and secrecy that was synonymous with Mossad's reputation.

The overarching challenge was that peace had once again given way to fighting and killing. With Hamas's relentless attacks, Israel was faced with a difficult dilemma, and the peace process seemed to hang in the balance. The struggle against Hamas, the rise of suicide bombings, and the Israeli government's response would prove to be a defining chapter in the complex history of the Israeli-Palestinian conflict.

The Poisoning of Hamas Leaders

Mossad faces immense pressure to achieve results in its campaign against Hamas leaders. Mossad agents compile a list of potential Hamas targets in Amman. However, their superiors are hesitant about carrying out an operation in Jordan.

Prime Minister Netanyahu is determined to strike at the heart of Hamas, starting with Kharid Mashal, the chief of Hamas's politburo. It's crucial that the operation leaves no trace of an Israeli strike to avoid implicating Jordan's government in the matter, especially in the midst of Palestinian uprisings in refugee camps.

The plan is to poison Mashal in broad daylight, making it appear as if he died of natural causes. The unit conducts experiments on unsuspecting individuals on the streets. Two operatives approach the target from behind, one distracts him while the other discreetly opens a can of cola, causing its contents to spray. The unsuspecting victim turns around, only to find a shaken can of cola, attributing the wetness to that.

Time is of the essence as Netanyahu seeks swift results. The operation takes an unexpected turn when the device used to administer the poison malfunctions. Chaos ensues as they attempt to evade capture. Mashal collapses, and his bodyguard quickly takes action, hailing a cab and pursuing the assassins.

A few minutes later, the assassins try to switch cars, but Mashal's bodyguard confronts them. Jordanian police arrive on the scene, and Mashal is rushed to the hospital in critical condition.

But as fate would have it, the excessive motivation of the operatives involved proved to be a double-edged sword. In a critical moment, Mashal emerged from the shadows, accompanied by her driver and two innocent children. Despite the explicit instructions, the team decided to forge ahead with their mission.

In an instant, the situation spiraled into chaos. Mashal was critically injured, two Mossad agents were exposed and captured, and the fragile peace agreement with Jordan hung by a thread. The consequences were dire; a Palestinian uprising loomed on the horizon, and the Israeli government faced an agonizing decision.

Enter Ed Hussain, a key figure in the diplomatic quagmire. He knew that Mashal's death would spell disaster and force the execution of the captured agents. Desperate to salvage the situation, a risky deal was struck with Hussein, the leader of Jordan. The promise was simple: Mashal's life would be spared using an antidote, and the two operatives would be released.

Israel reluctantly agreed to save the life of a person they considered a terrorist, but this decision came at a tremendous cost. Diplomatic relations with Jordan were severely disrupted, and former Mossad deputy director Ephraim Halevi was summoned to address the crisis. Halevi, a trusted negotiator in the region, sought to rescue the fragile peace treaty with Jordan, a treaty more valuable than any single individual.

The region paid a high price for peace. The founder of Hamas, Sheikh Raisin, was released from prison as a concession to Jordan to appease the Palestinian population. Khalid Mashao, a prominent figure, took the reins as the new leader of Hamas in waiting, ushering in an era of uncertainty.

The Mossad's operation, intended to weaken Hamas and curb suicide attacks, had the opposite effect. In September 2000, the Islamists unleashed the second Intifada, leading to a surge in suicide attacks and a severe challenge to Israeli intelligence agencies. The region was left grappling with the consequences of a mission gone awry, where the pursuit of peace had led to unexpected turmoil.

In the shadowy world of espionage, where the balance between success and catastrophe teetered on a knife's edge, the repercussions of this operation echoed through the annals of history, reminding us that the pursuit of peace can exact a heavy toll.

CHAPTER 24:
UNLEASHED FURY

*Mossad's Struggle Against
Unseen Enemies*

In the tumultuous aftermath of September 2000, a new storm gathered on the horizon as Islamist forces unleashed the second Intifada against Israel. The tumultuous sounds of conflict seemed to reverberate in the very air, and the number of suicide attacks surged, creating a landscape of fear and uncertainty.

In the shadows of this chaos, the once-proud institutions of Israeli military intelligence and Shin Bet found themselves in dire straits. They were facing perhaps the lowest point in their history. The relentless wave of suicide attacks had overwhelmed their capabilities, leaving them reeling and seemingly powerless to deal with the mounting threat.

As Ami Ayalon, who was the chief of the Shin Bet at the time, lamented, "We did not supply the citizens of Israel the shield they deserved." The protectors had faltered, and the citizens of Israel were left exposed to a menacing foe.

The Iman Fiasco, an operation gone awry, plunged Mossad into its most profound crisis to date. The once hard-hitting secret service now seemed vulnerable and shaken to its core. The fallout from this mission failure cast a dark shadow over the agency, leaving it at a crossroads, struggling to redefine its mission and purpose.

But adversity never comes singly, and after the turn of the millennium, a new, formidable adversary emerged on the scene: Iran. Mossad had to reset its sights as the Islamic Republic of Iran, viewing Israel as its sworn enemy, stepped onto the stage. Excluded from all peace-seeking efforts in the Middle East, Iran sought retribution through covert means.

To respond to their exclusion and express their disdain for the peace process, Iran began to increase its material aid to groups like Hamas and the Palestine Islamic Jihad. Their message was clear: if they couldn't be part of the process, they would undermine it. It was a warning that did not go unheeded.

Iran orchestrated a network among Israel's enemies, building close connections with Bashar Assad's regime in Syria, providing support to the Shiite Hezbollah militia in Lebanon through arms, money, and fighters. Even the Sunni Islamists in the occupied territories received aid from Tehran. It was a surprising alliance of convenience, transcending the historical divide between Sunni and Shiite Islam.

Despite their deep-seated differences, the confessional dispute seemed insignificant in the face of their shared objective – the fight against Israel. In the grand scheme of things, their common enemy took precedence over ancient divisions.

In 2002, Mossad witnessed a changing of the guard. Maya Dagan assumed the mantle of leadership, bringing a military background and a vision that would reshape the Secret Service. To Dagan, the primary adversary was clear: Iran. Under his leadership, Mossad underwent a fundamental transformation, moving from a talkative agency to one of action. Dagan's tenure marked a shift towards action-based, clear operations, setting the stage for a new chapter in Mossad's relentless pursuit of national security and global stability.

The Iron Fist: Mossad's Pursuit of a Secure Israel

In the turbulent landscape of espionage, Eliyahu Dagan, often called Madagan, emerged as the director of Mossad with a reputation for being robust and relentless. His leadership brought about a significant shift in the agency, reinvigorating it with a new sense of purpose. Dagan was resolute, declaring, "Stop all the talking; we're about actions, not words." Under his stewardship, Mossad transitioned from a place of soft diplomacy and covert chatter into an organization focused on action-driven, clear-cut operations. For eight years, Dagan steered Mossad towards this transformation, setting the stage for a new era of effectiveness.

Gone were the days of long-term undercover missions that yielded intangible results. Mossad agents were now expected to deliver tangible outcomes, and data was evaluated based on their immediate benefit to short-term operations.

Dagan set two primary objectives for Mossad. First, the agency was tasked with dismantling the anti-Israeli network that lurked behind the veil of terrorism. Second, and of even greater significance, was the relentless pursuit of dismantling Iran's burgeoning nuclear program. Since the late 1990s, Mossad had been keenly aware of Iran's nuclear facilities, which were officially claimed to serve civilian purposes. However, Israel viewed this potential nuclear capability in the hands of an adversary as a severe threat.

When Dagan assumed office, Mossad analysts estimated that Iran could possess nuclear weapons within a few years, spelling mortal danger for the region. Israel, with a history of thwarting nuclear ambitions among its neighbors, understood the catastrophic potential that even a few atomic bombs could unleash. For decades, Israel had maintained secrecy about its own nuclear program in the Negev Desert, only acknowledging its existence in 1986, revealing that the reactor had been producing weapons-grade plutonium since the 1960s.

In a collaborative effort, Mossad and another secret service were tasked with collecting the necessary data to safeguard Israel's status as the sole nuclear power in the Middle East. It was imperative to ensure that the balance of power remained in Israel's favor.

Mossad's commitment to this objective was evident when, in the early 1980s, Iraq's dictator, Saddam Hussein, began constructing a reactor with French support. Mossad initially sought to stall the program through diplomatic pressure and sabotage. However, Israel's government ultimately ordered an airstrike on the site in eastern Iraq, causing severe damage and sending a resounding message.

In 2007, Mossad was again jolted by alarming information, this time concerning a secret nuclear project in Syria. The response was immediate and decisive. Mossad recommended an airstrike, but this time, Israel chose to keep the operation covert, only revealing it to the world a decade later.

CHAPTER 25: SILENT WARFARE

Mossad's Battle Against
Nuclear Ambitions

The message sent by Israel through the 2007 attack on Syria's nuclear reactor was unambiguous: it would not tolerate any construction that could pose an existential threat to the state. This resolute stance was echoed throughout history, from the 1981 strike in Iraq to the covert mission in 2007, reinforcing Israel's commitment to preserving its security.

Yet, striking neighboring countries involved monumental risks, particularly when it came to Iran. Mossad warned that such actions could have incalculable consequences. Dagan, the director, had a firm conviction in deterring the need for overt military action. His preference lay in covert operations, unconventional alliances, and diplomacy behind the scenes.

He believed in focusing on the Arab world, even countries without official ties to Israel. Many Arab nations, particularly those with a Sunni majority, viewed Iran as equally dangerous as Israel. Collaborating with Israel presented an opportunity to counter Iran's nuclear threat. This change in approach faced fierce resistance within Mossad, but it also provided critical access to Iran, expanding the scope of Israel's intelligence operations.

Israel aimed to garner Western support to intensify pressure on Tehran. Explosive information, particularly on Iran's nuclear program, was discreetly shared with Mossad's Western counterparts. The Iranian threat was not confined to Israel alone; it had the potential to destabilize the world. Leaders understood the urgency of preventing Iran from mastering uranium enrichment, a pivotal step in their nuclear program.

Mossad also reached out to European partners, sharing vital intelligence. For years, they had monitored Iran's nuclear ambitions, a persistent concern that transcended time. Beyond the nuclear program, Mossad recognized the ominous nature of Iran's ballistic missile program. These weapons held the potential to inflict substantial harm and disruption, necessitating a comprehensive response.

Mossad advocated for international pressure, urging Iran to voluntarily abandon its nuclear ambitions. In this quest, a new weapon emerged – cyber sabotage. The choice of using cyber warfare was deliberate; it allowed for covert action without revealing its origin, preventing immediate retaliation and escalation.

Among these cyber operations, Stuxnet, a computer virus, took center stage. It crippled Iran's uranium enrichment plant, creating havoc within their nuclear infrastructure. Rumors circulated that this cyber attack was the result of covert collaboration between the CIA and Mossad. However, the true architects of Stuxnet remained concealed, and neither party was eager to claim responsibility.

In addition to digital warfare, Mossad leveraged an age-old method. Reflecting on history, Mossad's actions from four decades ago targeted German specialists working on an Egyptian missile project. Now, six scientists involved in Iran's nuclear program faced a similar fate, their lives abruptly and mysteriously extinguished.

Mossad's battle against nuclear ambitions showcased a multifaceted approach, balancing covert operations, intelligence-sharing, and the strategic use of cyber warfare. The agency's unwavering commitment to safeguarding Israel's security was evident, even in the face of complex geopolitical challenges.

The Lethal Chessboard: Mossad's Deadly Gambit

Mossad's relentless pursuit of its mission knew no bounds, employing both cutting-edge technology and age-old methods to achieve its objectives. The story begins four decades ago when Mossad targeted German specialists to thwart an Egyptian missile project. Fast forward to the present day, and the agency was once again compelled to resort to a lethal approach.

Six scientists involved in Iran's nuclear program were suddenly and mysteriously liquidated. The Iranians, feeling the weight of Mossad's shadow, invested extensive efforts in protecting their remaining scientists. They undertook rigorous screening of equipment brought into their nuclear project, fearing infiltration by bugs and viruses.

Intriguingly, the Iranians themselves inadvertently delayed their own project in their desperate bid to safeguard against Mossad's covert operations. Bureaucratic obstacles and security measures, designed to shield against external threats, ultimately played into Mossad's hands, affording Israel the precious gift of time.

More than 700 kilometers of walls and fences served as sentinels, protecting Israel from assassins lurking in the West Bank. Mossad's teams relentlessly hunted down the masterminds behind Hamas and Hezbollah reign of terror, and their actions bore fruit. The number of assassinations within Israel began to decline.

Lebanon's Hezbollah, no stranger to Mossad's tenacity, acknowledged that Israel had successfully assassinated one of its top leaders, Ahmad Marnier. The high-profile success marked yet another triumph for Mossad's relentless pursuit of justice.

However, the strategy of targeted killings was not without controversy, even within Israel. It had its roots in the early days of the Jewish underground in Palestine, a method designed to eliminate adversaries and enemies to save the lives of others. Since World War II, Israel had conducted more targeted killings than any other Western country, with estimates suggesting over 2,000 lives had been taken.

But the question remained: did this strategy truly help Israel in the long run? The answer was not straightforward. While it may have forced terrorist decision-makers to reconsider their tactics and kept them on the run, it was far from a comprehensive solution. The roots of the problem lay in political, economic, societal, cultural, and educational factors, and a more holistic approach was needed to address the underlying issues.

CHAPTER 26: CROSSROADS OF POWER

Mossad's Complex Mission

While Mossad's strategy of targeted killings has seen its share of successes, it has also sparked debates within the intelligence community. Many Israeli analysts share a common perspective – that while these actions buy time and disrupt immediate threats, they fail to address the underlying issue. Targeting today's Hamas fighters or those who fire missiles is only a temporary solution. The concern lies in the next generation, which may be larger in number, more desperate, and more determined to take drastic measures.

The way terrorists are fought is a decision that extends beyond Mossad's agents. It ultimately rests in the hands of Israel's voters and the majority of them favor a crackdown. Israel's approach to security is rooted in a historical context, which differs from much of the Western world's perspective.

In 2010, Mossad found itself in the midst of international outrage. Security cameras captured its agents liquidating a top Hamas functionary in Dubai. The incident caused an uproar, but within Israel, there was a show of solidarity for Mossad. Many citizens expressed support, some even offered their passports for use as covers.

The reverence for Mossad and Israeli intelligence in public opinion is striking. They are often regarded as the last line of defense, the protectors who risk their lives to keep the nation safe. However, the toll of this ongoing war is undeniable. Commemorative ceremonies in Tel Aviv honor the men and women who have fallen in the line of duty, serving as poignant reminders of the sacrifices made in a battle that shows no signs of ending.

In 2012, the nuclear dispute with Iran reached a critical juncture. Mossad's operations had succeeded in slowing down Iran's nuclear program, but they hadn't halted it. Israeli Prime Minister Benjamin Netanyahu, known for his unwavering stance, demanded radical measures against Iran while addressing the United Nations. He expressed a deep appreciation for Israel's intelligence agencies, acknowledging their role in saving lives.

Mossad's mission is far from simple; it operates in a complex and ever-changing world of espionage, where decisions carry immense consequences and the line between right and wrong is blurred by the shadows of security and national interest.

Mossad's Shifting Role

The pivotal question was not when Iran would acquire nuclear capabilities, but at what stage could the international community no longer prevent it from obtaining the bomb. Netanyahu, driven by a deep concern for Israel's security, was ready and willing to go to war against Iran. His fixation on the Iranian nuclear project was unmistakable, with Israel becoming Iran's primary target in the Middle East as a consequence.

Critics argued that Israel should not be Iran's central focus; they could have other targets and motives that didn't involve Israel. Still, Netanyahu's determination cast a long shadow over the region. Amidst this intense backdrop, Israel's intelligence services worked diligently to prevent an airstrike, leveraging their influence to stave off a conflict. Their strategy seemed to pay off in 2015 when Iran signed an agreement, curbing its nuclear ambitions in exchange for sanctions relief.

Hope flourished, but it was short-lived. In 2018, Mossad agents procured secret documents that allegedly contained proof of forbidden nuclear activities in Iran. Prime Minister Netanyahu made them public, declaring that "Iran lied." The revelation prompted U.S. President Donald Trump to terminate the nuclear agreement with Iran, signaling a major shift in the geopolitical landscape.

Mossad had, for years, played a significant role in helping policymakers find solutions to complex problems. However, the consequence of this success was that it allowed policymakers to sidestep more fundamental solutions to underlying issues.

Throughout its existence, Mossad had donned the dual hats of warmonger and peacemaker, guided by its mission to protect Israel at all costs. As the agency stood at a crossroads of power and influence, the complexities of the future remained daunting.

The world was in a state of flux, with the Middle East a crucible of shifting alliances, volatile geopolitics, and the relentless pursuit of security. The story of Mossad, as it continues to be written, is one of unwavering commitment, moral dilemmas, and the perpetual quest to ensure the survival of the state of Israel.

PART IV

CONCLUSION

*History to Present: A recall
of Mossad Journey*

In the heart of Dubai, a shadowy and deadly game unfolded in the year 2010. The unsuspecting victim, Mahmoud al-Mabu, a leader of the Palestinian terrorist organization Hamas, became the target of a covert operation that would send shockwaves through the world. A group of highly trained, covert agents, believed to be associated with Israel's secret service, the Mossad, descended upon the city. Their mission: to eliminate their target, Mahmoud al-Mabu, whose notoriety had made him a thorn in the side of Israel's national security.

The events that followed unfolded with the precision of a well-scripted thriller. These secret agents, far from being tourists, were on a deadly mission. They tracked their unsuspecting victim relentlessly, following him into the elevator of a luxurious Dubai hotel. Soon after, Mahmoud al-Mabu was discovered lifeless in his room, a victim of a meticulously planned murder. The evidence pointed clearly in one direction, the handiwork of Israel's secret service, the Mossad.

As swiftly as they had arrived, the assassins managed to slip away from Dubai, leaving behind a trail of suspicion and intrigue. Yet, despite the glaring clues, there was no official proof of their involvement. The operation was executed with such precision that it left no room for concrete attribution.

Israel has a long history of clandestine operations, making the Mossad renowned and feared worldwide. This incident in Dubai marked one of the most significant events in the region in the past 50 years, leaving both friends and foes of Israel in awe of the agency's capabilities. Within the Arab world, a deep-seated belief in conspiracies and myths about the Mossad is prevalent. The organization is often both glorified and demonized, used for political purposes. Some even assert that the Mossad had a hand in events like 9/11, although these claims lack concrete evidence.

The Mossad's mystique was not created intentionally but rather evolved as a byproduct of their strict policy of clandestine espionage and operational work. Over time, they realized that this mystique served them well. Any action attributed to the Mossad only served to enhance the aura surrounding the organization. Despite the speculation and intrigue, the Mossad is a relatively small organization, its exact number of personnel remaining a tightly guarded state secret. However, their daring operations and unwavering commitment to Israel's security have left an indelible mark on history.

From Inception to Operation Eichmann

The horrors of the Holocaust, etched deep into the collective memory of the Jewish people, laid the foundation for Israel's unwavering commitment to its security. The existential challenges it faced left no room for hesitation. The mantra was clear: "Rise and kill first." The guardians of this mission were the courageous men and women of the Mossad and other Israeli intelligence agencies.

Even before the establishment of the state of Israel, Jewish underground groups in Palestine recognized the power of precisely targeted secret operations. Their objective was clear: to establish a Jewish state in the heart of the Middle East.

In 1947, the United Nations passed the historic resolution to partition Palestine, laying the groundwork for the birth of Israel. This resolution, known as the UN Partition Plan, was adopted by 33 votes, and it marked a pivotal moment in the nation's history.

On May 14, 1948, David Ben-Gurion, a towering figure in Israel's history, proclaimed the independence of the new nation. However, this declaration was met with immediate hostility. That very night, an alliance of six Arab states launched an assault with the intent of crushing the nascent Jewish state. Against all odds, Israel emerged victorious, securing its place on the map of the world.

David Ben-Gurion, recognizing the need for an early warning system against further attacks, prioritized the establishment of effective intelligence services. The headquarters were set up in Tel Aviv, and from there, they orchestrated a worldwide network of intelligence gathering.

At the forefront of Israel's intelligence apparatus was Israel's Military Intelligence, tasked with spying on the enemy's armies and ensuring the nation's security. Alongside it was Shin Bet, the internal security service responsible for counter-espionage and anti-terror operations. Yet, perhaps the most famous of the trio was the Mossad, known for its secret activities abroad. Its mission was clear: to protect not only the citizens of Israel but also Jews around the world.

The Mossad's prowess, shrouded in secrecy, remained hidden until a spectacular operation brought it into the global spotlight. Adolf Eichmann, one of the key organizers of the Holocaust, managed to escape justice after the war, finding refuge in Buenos Aires under a false identity.

Word of his whereabouts reached the ears of the Israelis, and the Mossad swiftly swung into action. The operation, codenamed "Eichmann," was set in motion, with Mossad operative Rafi Eitan leading the charge. They established a covert hideout near Eichmann's residence.

Every day, a man returned home from work, commuting by bus, and the Mossad team observed him closely. The burning question was whether this seemingly ordinary man was, in fact, Adolf Eichmann, the perpetrator of unspeakable atrocities during the Holocaust. The operation to bring him to justice was underway, and the world would soon witness the audacious capabilities of the Mossad.

Operation Eichmann: Justice, Not Revenge

Every day, a man fitting their subject's description returned from work, commuting by bus. The Mossad team had to be certain - was this truly Adolf Eichmann? The tension in that moment was palpable. Eitan approached the man, speaking the words "momentito, Senor," and swiftly executed a double Nelson, forcing him to the ground.

Eichmann was apprehended, disoriented, and likely terrified. He was swiftly pushed into a waiting car. The agents' first question was simple, "What's your name?" To this, Eichmann replied, "Ricardo Clement." This was the name he had lived under in Argentina.

Moments later, Eichmann uttered the words that revealed the weight of his conscience, "I've been expecting this moment, day and night. I knew you Israelis would find me someday." His acknowledgment of guilt hung heavily in the air.

The agents had clear orders - Eichmann was to be put on a secret flight to Israel, where he would face justice for his crimes. Prime Minister David Ben-Gurion had recognized the immense implications of this case for the people of Israel. He was determined that Eichmann would be prosecuted in a trial that would stun the world.

Eichmann was brought to justice, entering the bulletproof prisoner's box at his trial. The message was clear - this was a pursuit of justice, not revenge. The trial was a coup for Israel and the Mossad, as Eichmann was ultimately sentenced to death in a landmark moment of modern times.

However, it's worth noting that Mossad director Isser Harel could have located Eichmann years before. While they had received information about his whereabouts, they hadn't initially recognized the potential of pursuing and bringing Nazi war criminals to justice. Other priorities took precedence. It was only after the fact that the magnitude of the operation's publicity and the myth it created became clear.

Through the abduction of Eichmann, the Mossad had laid the foundations of its own myth, sending a resounding message to Israel's enemies - their agents could strike anywhere, seeking justice for the horrors of the past.

This operation made the Jewish people proud. It conveyed a powerful message to the world: "You tried to annihilate us, but we're here. The Jewish people live and exist." Yet, in the complex world of intelligence, new and more recent threats would soon demand the Mossad's unwavering attention.

In the summer of 1962, Israel's arch-enemy, Egypt, proudly unveiled its new missile program, led by President Gamal Abdel

Nasser. The program aimed to unite Arab countries against the Jewish state, setting the stage for new challenges that Mossad's spies would have to confront.

The Shadows of Victory and the Birth of Fatah

The looming threat of an imminent attack by its Arab neighbors during the Six-Day War drove Israel to prepare for the worst. Israeli pilots took full advantage of the intelligence gleaned from the evaluation of Munir Redfa's MiG-21. In less than a week, Israeli forces had decisively beaten back the Arab armies, marking a stunning victory, made possible not least by invaluable intelligence.

The critical intelligence from a Mossad spy operating in the heart of Damascus played a significant role in Israel's victory. In the early 1960s, the Israelis had successfully infiltrated a top source in the Syrian capital. Eli Cohen, posing as a wealthy Arab businessman, had embedded himself within the highest circles of the Syrian regime. For years, he provided Mossad with vital war-related data on the Syrian military. However, his daring mission came to a tragic end in 1965 when he was captured and paid with his life. Despite this, his reports and information were instrumental in helping Israel win the Six-Day War, reshaping Israeli society and amplifying the myth of Israeli intelligence.

The post-war landscape saw Israel emerge as a regional power, with its territory expanding fourfold compared to its 1948 borders. For Israel, land equated to protection, and the young nation had secured its dominance. Yet, this newfound power sharpened the conflict between Arabs and Jews.

With the occupation of the last Arab-controlled territories in former Palestine, namely the Gaza Strip and the West Bank, tens of thousands of refugees found their hopes dashed. The dream of returning to their homeland remained elusive. Mossad realized the implicit dangers of this situation only belatedly.

Frustration festered in the refugee camps, especially among the younger generation of Palestinians. Mossad grew increasingly concerned about their radicalization. A new party, Fatah, emerged as the rallying point for resistance fighters. Fatah's ultimate goal was to liberate all of Palestine, an aim that directly challenged Israel's existence. The ranks of young Palestinians joining Fatah, along with its political arm, the Palestine Liberation Organization (PLO) led by Yasser Arafat, swelled. Their mission was to assert the rights of their people in the tumultuous Middle East.

The Israeli intelligence community was well aware of the Palestinian resistance, viewing it as a formidable challenge. The stage was set for a new chapter in the complex and often deadly conflict between Israelis and Palestinians. In the shadows of victory, the seeds of enduring conflict and resistance were sown, and the struggle for control of the region continued to intensify.

The Unyielding Challenge of the PLO: Munich 1972"

The Palestinian resistance, particularly through Fatah and its political arm, the Palestine Liberation Organization (PLO) led by Yasser Arafat, was gaining momentum with an explicit aim: to erase Israel from the map. Young Palestinians were increasingly joining the ranks of Fatah, driven by a fervent desire to assert the rights of their people in the Middle East.

The Israeli intelligence community viewed this gathering and the rise of Palestinian resistance as a formidable challenge. With Israeli control over the territories, they had significantly more resources at their disposal, including recruitment from the West Bank and Gaza Strip for covert operations. This Palestinian response by way of terror posed an entirely new challenge for

Mossad.

Arafat emerged as the prime target for Mossad due to his prominent role in the Palestinian resistance. However, he consistently evaded every attempt on his life. Recognizing the limitations of targeting him in the occupied territories, Arafat increasingly shifted his activities abroad, particularly to Europe, where a substantial Palestinian diaspora resided. In Europe, the PLO found allies among leftist circles, leveraging Western liberal environments to establish networks and recruit followers.

Mossad was initially hesitant to conduct operations in Europe. Abdallah al-Franji, who would later become the PLO representative in West Germany, led the Palestinian student movement in Frankfurt. Their activities, including organizing demonstrations and disseminating Palestinian symbols and slogans, received support from sympathetic European audiences.

Europe became a stage for radical actions by the PLO and its splinter groups, who carried out assaults to draw international attention to the Palestinian cause.

Then came the fateful year of 1972, and the Olympic Games in Munich were supposed to showcase post-war Germany as a liberal and peaceful nation. However, matters took a tragic turn on the morning of September 5th.

Palestinian guerrillas infiltrated the Olympic Village, launching an attack that resulted in the deaths of two members of the Israeli Olympic team and the taking of at least 13 hostages. Mossad had been alarmed by hints of a planned assault, though the information was vague. They faced the immense challenge of gathering accurate and timely intelligence to prevent a catastrophe.

The events in Munich marked a grim chapter in the ongoing conflict between Israelis and Palestinians. The world watched in horror as the tragedy unfolded, and Mossad's role in preventing such attacks would continue to be a pivotal aspect of their efforts to protect Israel's security.

Munich Olympics Tragedy: A Dark Day for Mossad

In the lead-up to the tragic events at the 1972 Munich Olympics, Mossad was alarmed by vague hints pointing to a planned assault. Intelligence was limited to a general sense that something was amiss. In the world of intelligence, having accurate and timely information is crucial. However, in the case of Munich, the critical intelligence they needed was missing.

The situation took a dire turn when Palestinian terrorists took nine athletes hostage. Their demands were clear: the release of over 200 of their comrades from Israeli prisons, or they threatened to kill the hostages. German security forces, unfortunately, proved ill-equipped to handle such a crisis. There were no specialized teams trained for an emergency of this magnitude, unlike in Israel.

Prime Minister Golda Meir rejected the terrorists' demands but offered to send help for a rescue attempt. It was a race against time, and Mossad's director was compelled to watch helplessly as ordinary police officers, dressed in plain clothes, attempted to position themselves for a rescue operation. To make matters worse, television cameras captured every move, providing the terrorists with a live feed of the police's actions. Eventually, the rescue operation had to be called off.

As the hostage-takers grew increasingly nervous, they demanded to be flown out of Munich. A crisis team decided to feign compliance with their demand, arranging for two helicopters to transport the terrorists and their hostages to a nearby airbase, where the police planned to strike. However, none of the officers involved in the operation were trained snipers, and they found themselves ill-prepared for the task.

The rescue attempt ultimately failed, with the terrorists opening fire on the helicopters, causing one to burst into flames. Tragically, all the Israelis on board died, and the hostages in the second helicopter were shot and killed by the terrorists. None of the athletes survived. In the ensuing gunfight with the police, five of the eight terrorists lost their lives.

This devastating incident marked a dark day for Mossad and Israel. Twenty-seven years after the Holocaust, Jews had once again fallen victim to violence on German soil. The Munich Olympics tragedy was a somber reminder of the ongoing conflict and the high stakes involved in protecting Israel's security. It also underlined the need for Mossad to be prepared for any contingency, even on foreign soil, as the shadow of terror continued to loom.

Mossad's Crusade Against Terror: Rise and Kill First

In the aftermath of the Holocaust, Jews faced persecution even on foreign soil, where not even Mossad could protect them. A few weeks after the tragic events in Munich, a Palestinian Terror Commando attempted to enforce the release of the three surviving hostage-takers from Munich. They hijacked a Lufthansa jet, and shockingly, the German government acquiesced to their demands, releasing the assassins. In the Arab world, they were celebrated as heroes, a grievous slap in the face for Israel. It became increasingly evident that the Jewish state could only rely on itself.

Prime Minister Golda Meir was under immense pressure. It was election time, and the country yearned for revenge. In this charged atmosphere, Golda Meir gave Mossad the go-ahead for a relentless crusade against terror. The Olympic Games terrorist operation had a profound impact on Israeli policy, as it led the Israeli cabinet to grant Mossad the authority to eliminate Palestinian operatives in Europe, even if it meant violating international rules and laws. They had concluded that if Israel didn't take on this grim task, no one else would. The directive was clear: "Rise and kill first."

Mossad activated a small team code-named "Kidon," whose mission was secret liquidations abroad. These agents were dispatched to track down and eliminate the masterminds of terror. Their operations would come to define Mossad's image for decades to come.

However, Kidon was just the spearhead of a more extensive intelligence service. Mossad's inner structure was a closely guarded state secret. Yet, there was mention of eight departments within Mossad.. Cachet specialized in collecting information through wiretapping, surveillance, and burglaries. However, the largest department was Summit, responsible for gathering information from human sources and maintaining a vast global network of informants.

Mossad's Relentless Pursuit: Unintended Consequences and a Changing Strategy

The campaign against Palestinian terrorists, launched in October 1972, was driven by a desire for revenge, but it also had the primary goal of preventing further acts of terror against Israel. Mossad recognized that to safeguard their nation and people, they needed to take all necessary measures, utilizing cunning and precision in their operations. The objective was clear: to ensure their adversaries could not question their presence.

The killings orchestrated by Mossad served as a visible warning to the PLO and other Palestinian organizations. High-ranking PLO members reacted by seeking refuge in Arab countries. As a response, Mossad extended its list of targets to include members residing in Western Europe, where Israeli agents could operate more freely.

One notable target was student leader Abdallah al-franji, who was suspected to have ties with the Munich assassins. However, al-franji was arrested by German police, along with hundreds of other Arabs, and faced imminent expulsion. His time in jail actually saved his life, as the tough stance against Arabs taken by the authorities after the Munich massacre made him less of a priority.

Al-franji eventually relocated to Algeria to coordinate the PLO's European sections from a remote position. Despite the distance, Mossad continued its pursuit of him.

The PLO retaliated against Mossad's relentless campaign. An incident in Algeria saw a horrific explosion that injured PLO representatives. Mossad's counterterrorism campaign proved highly successful, leading to the assassination of 14 Palestinians within a year.

However, the Kidon assassinations met an unfortunate turn in July 1973 during an operation in Lillehammer, Norway. In a regrettable mix-up, Israeli agents mistakenly killed a Moroccan waiter whom they had mistaken for Ali Hassan Salameh, the alleged mastermind of the Munich attack. To compound the problem, these agents were apprehended by Norwegian police. The aftermath of this operation led to the exposure of communication channels and agent hideouts all over Europe, marking a significant disaster for the Secret Service.

The vendetta against the PLO came to a preliminary end, as the PLO leadership decided to shift their attacks to the occupied territories, believing that terrorist actions in the West were harming their image. However, not all factions within the Palestinian resistance adhered to this directive, and assaults and hostage-taking operations in Europe persisted. Mossad remained vigilant, continuing its pursuit of those who posed a threat to Israel, demonstrating their unwavering commitment to safeguarding the nation and its people.

The Oslo Accords and a New Chapter

By 1987, nearly two decades had passed since Israel's occupation of the West Bank and the Gaza Strip. During this time, Israel had struggled to quell Palestinian violence, and the lack of prospects for a better future had fueled frustration. This frustration reached a boiling point in the occupied territories, leading to the eruption of the Intifada, the people's uprising. The Palestinian streets were filled with anger and resistance, catching Israel off guard.

Throughout this period, Mossad's operations against the PLO leadership were primarily focused on foreign countries, where many PLO leaders were in hiding. This was a classic domain of Mossad's activity. In Tunis, agents from Mossad and the Israeli military were tasked with liquidating the alleged mastermind behind the uprising, Abu Jihad.

However, as time passed, it became increasingly evident that the PLO leadership in distant locations wasn't solely responsible for the uprising. Targeting these leaders didn't bring an end to the Intifada, and the demands for a diplomatic solution in Israel were growing louder.

In 1993, Israelis and Palestinians finally met on neutral ground in Oslo to negotiate peace proposals. After decades of mutual violence, this marked a significant step towards potential peace. However, Israel's secret services, including Mossad, were conspicuously left out of the process. The decision to exclude them was made by Prime Minister Yitzhak Rabin, and Mossad's top brass only became aware of the Oslo talks through their own channels of information.

Their knowledge of the ongoing negotiations was minimal, and Rabin's approach was dismissive. The prime minister chose to keep his cards close to his chest, leaving Mossad in the dark about the details of the negotiations. Rabin had opted for a path that he believed didn't require Mossad's advice or involvement, which was a notable departure from the past.

Rabin eventually concluded an agreement with the Palestinians. As part of the Oslo Accords, the West Bank and the Gaza Strip were returned to Palestinian autonomy. In exchange, the PLO agreed to cease its attacks on Israel. This historic development marked a new chapter in the longstanding Israeli-Palestinian conflict, but it also signaled a shift in the role of Israel's secret services, including Mossad, in the changing landscape of diplomacy and conflict resolution.

Shadows of Deceit

The sun dipped low over the horizon, casting long shadows across the streets of Jerusalem. The air hung heavy with tension, as if the very city itself held its breath, awaiting the inevitable storm.

Prime Minister Benjamin Netanyahu sat in his office, the weight of his responsibility pressing down on him. The room was suffused with an air of urgency, a palpable sense that time was running out. The recent surge in Hamas activity had thrust Israel into a perilous dance of diplomacy and danger. Netanyahu's steely gaze fixated on the list before him, a list that held the names of those deemed a threat to his nation's security. The leaders of Hamas, elusive shadows in the shifting sands of Jordan, taunted him from afar.

Mossad, Israel's shadowy guardian, was tasked with the impossible. They were to strike at the heart of Hamas, to cut off the serpent's head, and yet the mission was fraught with peril. Jordan's wary government watched like a hawk, fearing the tinderbox of Palestinian camps erupting into chaos. The plan was audacious, to poison Misha, the enigmatic leader of Hamas, under the harsh glare of day. But the execution had to be flawless, leaving no trace, no whisper of Israeli involvement. It was a gambit that could tip the scales, but it was a gambit they had to take.

As the sun sank lower, casting long, stretching fingers of darkness through the city, Netanyahu knew that time was not on his side. The clock ticked down, each second a heartbeat echoing the urgency of the task at hand. In the covert chambers of Mossad, agents moved like phantoms, their faces masked by shadows, their every move calculated, rehearsed. The weight of the nation's hopes rested on their shoulders, and failure was not an option.

The night before the operation, Jerusalem held its breath. The streets were quiet, but beneath the surface, a current of anticipation pulsed through the city's veins. The moon hung low, casting an ethereal glow over the ancient stones, as if the very heavens watched in judgment. And then, as dawn painted the horizon with hues of crimson and gold, the operation was set into motion. The streets of Amman, Jordan, became the stage for a deadly dance of shadows and deceit.

The agents moved with precision, their nerves steel, their senses honed. Misha, the target, walked unknowingly into the web they had woven. In the heart of daylight, amidst the bustling city, the deed was done. A lethal dose administered, a chapter closed. As the news spread, shockwaves rippled through the region. The leader of Hamas, the symbol of resistance, lay still and silent. The world watched, breathless, as the implications of this audacious act unfurled.

But the game was far from over. In the dark corners of the labyrinthine struggle, new players lurked, waiting to seize their moment. The specter of Hamas still loomed, its tendrils reaching out, its fanatical vision undimmed. In the heart of Jerusalem, Prime Minister Netanyahu knew that this was but a battle, not the war. The shadows of deceit would continue to dance, the stakes ever higher, the risks ever greater. As the sun set once more over the ancient city, casting its long shadows, a tense calm settled. The world held its breath, waiting for the next move in this deadly game of shadows.

Echoes of Struggle

In the aftermath of the ill-fated operation, a pall of tension settled over the region. The plan to covertly neutralize Misha had careened off course, leaving a trail of exposed secrets in its wake. Netanyahu's demand for swift results had driven Mossad to take risks, but those risks had come at a steep cost. As the operation unraveled, agents found themselves face-to-face with unexpected obstacles. Martial, the elusive target, stood before them, shielded by the innocence of his children and the vigilant presence of a bodyguard.

Yet, determination forged their path. They pressed forward, the weight of their mission heavy on their shoulders. The audacious scheme played out, a can of cola becoming an unwitting accomplice in the elaborate ruse. As the spray settled, the realization dawned on the unsuspecting victim, but it was too late. The die was cast, and the consequences would reverberate far beyond this moment.

Escape proved elusive, as Mashal's bodyguard moved swiftly to apprehend the agents. In the ensuing struggle, the mission spiraled further out of control, leaving Mossad's operatives exposed and in custody. Back in Israel, the repercussions of the operation reached a boiling point. King Hussein of Jordan was faced with a stark ultimatum. With Mashal's life hanging in the balance, the specter of a Palestinian uprising loomed large.

In a reluctant accord, a deal was struck. The antidote, the thin thread between life and death, was administered, sparing Mashal's life. In return, the captured agents were released, but the scars of this diplomatic gamble ran deep. Israel paid a heavy toll for this precarious peace. The release of Sheikh Yassin, a figurehead of Hamas, to Jordan's soil was a bitter pill to swallow. It was a concession meant to placate the Palestinian population there, a nod to the delicate balance of power.

Yet, the storm continued to brew. Khalid Mashal stepped into the void left by Misha, poised to lead Hamas in its relentless campaign against Israel. The attacks persisted, an unyielding tide of violence. Then came September 2000, the unleashing of the second intifada. The ranks of suicide bombers swelled, and the very foundations of Israeli security apparatus quaked under the onslaught.

Mossad, Israeli military intelligence, and Shin Bet found themselves in a precarious position. Their capacities strained to the limit, they grappled with an enemy that seemed one step ahead, a threat they were ill-prepared to face. Amidst this tumultuous period, Mossad found itself at a crossroads. The Iran debacle had left scars, but a new opportunity emerged on the horizon. The extremist rhetoric emanating from Tehran painted Israel as the embodiment of evil, a force to be eradicated.

Excluded from the realm of peace initiatives, Iran lurked in the shadows, casting a long, ominous shadow over the fragile stability of the region. Their intentions were clear: to undermine any semblance of progress, to sow discord, and to fan the flames of conflict. As the pages of history turned, the struggle for peace in the Middle East seemed destined to be forever entwined with the relentless pursuit of those who sought its undoing. The echoes of strife reverberated through the ages, a testament to the enduring resilience of those who dared to hope for a brighter future.

Shadows of the Atom Bomb

In the clandestine corridors of geopolitics, Iran loomed as an ominous figure, casting Israel as the embodiment of evil, the very Satan incarnate. Excluded from peace initiatives, Iran chose a path of defiance, vowing to undermine any attempts at reconciliation. Iran wove a sinister web among Israel's adversaries, nurturing ties with Bashar Assad's regime in Syria and bolstering the militant Hezbollah in Lebanon. Even the radical Sunni Islamists in the occupied territories found solace in Tehran's support.

In 2002, a new guardian took the helm of Mossad: Mayor Dagan. His gaze was fixed squarely on Iran, recognizing it as the most formidable foe. Dagan was known for his unyielding resolve, an uncompromising figure who breathed fresh vigor into the agency. As Dagan assumed command, Mossad's analysts sounded a dire warning: Iran's nuclear ambitions were fast approaching fruition. The specter of a nuclear-armed Iran hung heavy, a threat that Israel could ill afford.

To halt Iran's nuclear juggernaut, Mossad embraced cyber warfare. The Stuxnet virus emerged as a digital weapon of devastating potential, wreaking havoc on Iran's uranium enrichment facilities. Whispers of clandestine collaboration between the CIA and Mossad shrouded the operation. Yet, the old ways endured. Mossad's operatives, shadows in the night, struck with ruthless precision. Scientists vital to Iran's nuclear pursuits met their end, a testament to Mossad's enduring resolve.

Israel fortified its borders, erecting walls of concrete and steel, a fortress against the ever-looming threat. The toll of the struggle was etched in these formidable defenses, a stark reminder of the sacrifices made for security. High-ranking terrorists met their reckoning at the hands of Mossad's agents. It was a calculated calculus, a belief that in eliminating adversaries, lives were saved. Controversial even within Israel, it was a doctrine forged in the crucible of necessity.

Yet, as the operations surged, a sobering truth emerged. Intelligence agencies, for all their might, were but one facet of a complex problem. Terrorism was a Hydra, its roots embedded in political, economic, and societal ills. To merely snip at its branches was to court perpetual conflict.

Mossad, for all its triumphs, stood at a precipice. Its legendary status rested on past glories, but the world was shifting. New threats, nebulous and unpredictable, lurked on the horizon, impervious to the old tactics.

The echoes of covert operations resonated through history, a testament to the indomitable spirit of those who fought in the shadows. But as the world hurtled forward, the question loomed: could Mossad adapt, evolve, and prevail against an ever-changing landscape of peril? The answer remained shrouded in the uncertainties of the future.

◆ ◆ ◆

BOOKS BY THIS AUTHOR

Beyond Politics: Vivek Ramaswamy's Vision For A New America

"Beyond Politics" is a thought-provoking exploration of Vivek Ramaswamy's visionary blueprint for a future that transcends political divisions. In this book, Ramaswamy challenges the status quo and calls for unity in divisive times. He advocates for a return to core American principles, emphasizing individual liberty, free-market capitalism, and self-governance. With a focus on education, healthcare, the environment, and economic development, Ramaswamy presents innovative solutions that challenge conventional political ideologies.

The Great Recession: The Shocking Truth About The 2008 Financial Crisis

Are you tired of the constant financial pain, the nagging agitation that comes with money worries, and the overwhelming feeling that your financial life is spinning out of control? Look no further. "Mastering Personal Finance" is your beacon of hope, guiding you towards a brighter financial future.

www.ingramcontent.com/pod-product-compliance
Lightning Source LLC
Chambersburg PA
CBHW070815260726
48660CB00005B/1856